Write
Right!

Write

A Desktop Digest of Punctuation, Grammar, and Style

Right!

Fourth Edition

Jan Venolia

Author of *Better Letters, Rewrite Right!,* and *Kids Write Right!*

Ten Speed Press
BERKELEY • TORONTO

Ten Speed Press
Box 7123
Berkeley, California 94707
www.tenspeed.com

Distributed in Australia by Simon & Schuster Australia, in Canada by Ten Speed
Press Canada, in New Zealand by Southern Publishers Group, in South Africa by
Real Books, in Southeast Asia by Berkeley Books, and in the United Kingdom and
Europe by Airlift Book Company.

Cover design by Paul Kepple
Book design by Tasha Hall
Copyediting by Suzanne Byerley
Illustrations by Ellen Sasaki

Library of Congress Cataloging-in-Publication Data
  Venolia, Jan.
      Write right! : a desktop digest of punctuation, grammar, and style /
  Jan Venolia.—4th ed.
        p. cm.
      Includes bibliographical references and index.
      ISBN 1-58008-328-5
      1. English language—Grammar—Handbooks, manuals, etc. 2. English
  language—Punctuation—Handbooks, manuals, etc. 3. English language—
  Style—Handbooks, manuals, etc. I. Title.
  PE1112 .V4   2001
  428.2—dc21

                                        2001003524

Printed in the United States of America
First printing, this edition, 2001

1 2 3 4 5 6 7 8 9 10 — 05 04 03 02 01

> *Words are the only tools you will be given.*
> *Learn to use them with originality and care.*
> *Value them for their strength and diversity.*
> *And also remember that somebody*
> *out there is listening.*
> —William Zinsser
>
> *Amen.*
> —Jan Venolia

Writing is easy. All you have to do is cross out the wrong words.
—Mark Twain

Contents

Why All the Fuss?

> Our language is an invaluable resource,
> as much a part of our heritage as forests,
> wildlife, and waters. —Paul Lovinger

Does good writing matter any more? In an e-commerce environment, do you still need to know how to create an effective sentence? Absolutely! Magazines, newspapers, and books are written words, whether in electronic or print form. What emerges from fax machines and appears on computer screens is writing, not speech. Businesses still need to "put it in writing." Furthermore, what's written needs to be clear and concise. That's where punctuation and grammar come in.

On the job or at school, you probably have to write—fast *and* well. You need to know how to choose the words that best convey your ideas and how to organize them for maximum effect. Can you rely on software to improve your writing? It helps. You can easily revise text, experiment with format, and find typos (though spell-checkers have definite limitations). But grammar-checkers are more annoying than useful. A concise handbook like *Write Right!* remains your best bet.

But what *is* good writing? And who says so? Who decides which changes in language are acceptable and which are to be rejected? Described as "usage wars," this subject is hotly debated in language and education circles.

On one side, the combatants declare that what constitutes good English should not be determined by arbitrary and archaic rules but by how the language has evolved. They cite the living nature of language to justify accepting change of all kinds. They study everyday speech and writing, and what they determine to be the norms are then deemed acceptable. Anyone who disagrees is considered to be elitist.

Trying to hold the line against this "anything goes" approach are those who believe that effective communication adheres to certain rules. Those rules make it more likely that written words will be understood. Clear writing is not seen as "archaic" but just good policy.

By now, you have probably deduced which side I'm on in these language wars. I, in turn, am able to make some assumptions about you. You are reading these lines, so I presume you want sound guidance in the matter of writing well.

I will not advise you that the language you hear on the street or even on the evening news is what you should emulate. Instead, I will draw upon judgments accumulated over decades of writing, of reading, and of studying the rules of clear and effective writing.

My judgments are grounded in the belief that making the reader's job easier is in the interests of reader and writer alike.

By making the reader's job easier, you show respect. You show consideration. At the same time, you improve the odds of being understood and thus of communicating what you want to communicate. True, an ill-formed, confusing sentence can usually be teased apart and understood—eventually. But why waste the reader's time trying to guess what you mean? Clarity and precision are always desirable.

Be forewarned, while you're improving your writing, I want you to rediscover the English language and rally to its defense. Its richness and variety are under siege. When *disinterested* becomes synonymous with *uninterested* and *dilemma* with *predicament*, we lose important tools for expressing ourselves. If wrong words proliferate, then *hone* replaces *home*, *staunch* crowds out *stanch*, and we encounter hybrids like *doubtlessly*, a kissing cousin of the redundant *irregardless*. Theodore Bernstein, author of *The Careful Writer*, suggests that accepting this degradation of language is the equivalent of declaring a crime legal when it has been committed often enough.

Concerned about this loss of richness in our language, I've expanded the sections on usage and style in *Write Right!* Alas, many of the examples of errors that I've included come from magazines, newspapers, and even books—publications that had been read by someone who was paid to catch such errors. Even so, the best antidote for the epidemic of wrong words is to read widely but with an informed eye. I propose to help you become informed.

Write Right! covers the common errors writers make in punctuation and grammar. Avoiding those errors means you're off to a good start. But lifeless prose and sloppy usage are greater threats to good writing than misuse of an apostrophe, so the rest of the book addresses those problems as well.

PART ONE, *The Basics*, provides a review of grammatical terms. Though not ends in themselves, the terms do help you understand the rules I've included in this book. Chapter 1, "Coming to Terms with Terms," defines the eight parts of speech and describes the elements that make up sentences. It goes into additional detail for the two trickiest parts of speech, verbs and pronouns.

PART TWO, *The Tools of Writing*, covers grammar, punctuation, and copyediting. Refer to Chapter 2, "Grammatical Guidelines," with questions about agreement of subject and verb or how to avoid dangling modifiers. Chapter 3, "Punctuation Pointers," tells you where to put apostrophes and commas, while Chapter 4, "Copyediting Considerations," helps you add a professional gloss in such matters as capitalization, italics, and treatment of numbers.

PART THREE, *The Craft of Writing*, considers the final product. Chapter 5, "Words," takes a look at the words we use and how we use them. Its list of tricky words sorts out confusing pairs like *affect* and *effect* and brings you up to date on the acceptability of such words as *contact* and *hopefully*. Chapter 6, "Style," helps you root out ho-hum writing. After all, a sentence can be grammatically correct, properly punctuated, and still be tedious. You want to invigorate your writing as well.

The final section in the book, *Resources*, includes a glossary, bibliography, list of frequently misspelled words, and the addresses of some interesting Web sites.

As in previous editions of *Write Right!*, the rules are illustrated with quotations that were chosen to edify and amuse. Throughout, Ellen Sasaki's whimsical drawings keep us from taking ourselves, and our rules, too seriously.

Write Right! answers the questions about writing that come up most often in your work or studies. Keep it next to your keyboard or tucked in a desk drawer for ready reference. If you need help with a more advanced level of revising, refer to *Rewrite Right! Your Guide to Perfectly Polished Prose.* (See the bibliography.)

The more you practice good writing, the easier it becomes. Enjoy the process!

> *By our choices we make usage, good or bad.*
> *Let us then try to make good choices, and*
> *guard and praise our lovely language and try*
> *to be worthy of her.*—Morris Bishop

Part One
The Basics

1 Coming to Terms with Terms

> *Words are all we have.*
> —Samuel Beckett

Recently, a friend was fretting that she didn't remember what predicates were. I assured her that you don't have to be able to define a grammatical term in order to use it correctly. Terminology is just a tool—a handy way to refer to the elements of writing. It's a lot easier to say "predicate" than "a word or group of words that makes a statement or asks a question about the subject of a sentence."

If you have only a few holes in your grammar vocabulary, skip this chapter now and refer to it as needed. But if you want a thorough review of grammatical terms, begin right here.

Parts of Speech

Let's start by defining the eight parts of speech: noun, verb, adjective, adverb, conjunction, preposition, pronoun, and interjection. Then we'll look at how they function in sentences.

Noun: *n.,* a word that names a person, place, thing, quality, or act.

> The <u>wise</u> talk because they have something to say; <u>fools</u> because they have to say something.—Plato

 If you can put *a, an,* or *the* in front of a word, it's a noun.

Proper nouns identify specific persons, places, or things.

> Taj Mahal, Halloween, Aristotle, Cairo, Titanic

Common nouns are ordinary, run-of-the-mill nouns.

> kitten, bravery, shoelace, letter, honesty

Nouns can be concrete (*toenail, tinsel, tomahawk*) or abstract (*duty, diligence, danger*).

Verb: *v.,* a word that expresses action (*to win*), occurrence (*to happen*), or mode of being (*am, was, are* and the other forms of *to be*).

> You <u>climb</u> a long ladder until you <u>see</u> over the roof, or over the clouds. You <u>are writing</u> a book.—Annie Dillard

A sentence isn't complete without a verb, so it's important to be able to recognize them. (See p. 12.)

Helping verbs (also called **auxiliary verbs**) save you the trouble of changing the main verb to show past, present, and future tense. The twenty-three helping verbs are *can, could, would, should, do, does, did, has, have, had, may, might,* *must, shall,* and *will* plus the eight forms of *to be* (*am, are, be, been, being, is, was, were*).

> In what other language <u>could</u> your nose run and your feet smell.—Richard Lederer

> <u>May</u> your left ear wither and fall into your right pocket. —Ancient curse

Linking verbs, as their name suggests, provide the connection between the subject and the noun or adjective in the predicate.

> Opportunities always <u>look</u> bigger going than coming.

Pronoun: *pron.,* a word that takes the place of a noun. Examples are *they, it, you, who,* and *she.*

> <u>It's</u> so beautifully arranged on the plate, <u>you</u> know that <u>someone's</u> fingers have been all over <u>it</u>.—Julia Child

> Experience is a wonderful thing. <u>It</u> enables <u>you</u> to recognize a mistake when <u>you</u> see <u>it</u> again.

What the pronoun replaces is called its **antecedent.** Pronouns are particularly helpful if the antecedent is long or complicated: leftover macaroni and cheese; an inner-city after-school program; a dense, nutty-flavored, unassuming wine.

Adjective: *adj.,* a word or group of words that modifies a noun or pronoun.

> <u>purple</u> possum, <u>hysterical</u> hippopotamus, <u>slimy</u> salamander

Adjectives are called modifiers because they limit or restrict the words they are modifying. Not just any possum, but the *purple* possum.

> <u>Bad</u> times have a <u>scientific</u> value; these are occasions a <u>good</u> learner would not miss.—Ralph Waldo Emerson

The adjectives *a*, *an*, and *the* are called **articles.** When you see an article, you know that a noun is coming.

Adverb: *adv.*, a word or group of words that modifies a verb, adjective, or other adverb. Adverbs answer such questions as when (*now*), where (*aloft*), how much (*very*), to what extent (*extremely*), and in what manner (*deftly*).

Both adjectives and adverbs are modifiers, but they modify different kinds of words. Adjectives modify nouns or pronouns; adverbs modify verbs, adjectives, or other adverbs.

> Age is a <u>very</u> <u>high</u> <u>price</u> to pay for maturity.
>   adv. adj. noun

The adverb *very* modifies the adjective *high*; the adjective *high* modifies the noun *price*.

Conjunction: *conj.*, a word that connects other words, phrases, and clauses.

> peaches <u>and</u> cream   shaken <u>but</u> not stirred

Coordinating conjunctions (*and, but, or, nor, for, so, yet*) connect terms of equal grammatical value.

Blessed are they who can laugh at themselves _for_ they shall never cease to be amused.

Correlative conjunctions are coordinating conjunctions that come in pairs: _either/or, not only/but also, both/and, whether/or._

> _I figure you have the same chance of winning the lottery <u>whether</u> you play <u>or</u> not._—Fran Lebowitz

> _Publishing literary novels is like sailing a small craft; <u>either</u> you catch the wind <u>or</u> you paddle very hard._—Nan Talese

Subordinating conjunctions connect clauses of unequal grammatical value: an independent and a dependent clause. An independent clause can stand by itself as a complete sentence; a dependent clause requires an independent clause to complete its meaning. Subordinating conjunctions include _until, since, before, as, if, when, although, because, as long as,_ and _after._

> <u>If</u> you look like your passport picture, you probably need the trip.

> Always yield to temptation, <u>because</u> it may not pass by your way again.

Preposition: _prep._, a word that shows the relationship between its object (the noun or pronoun following the preposition) and other words in a sentence.

The most common prepositions show direction (_through_ the looking glass), time (_during_ her term of office), and possession (_with_ my friends). Less obvious examples of prepositions include _notwithstanding, concerning,_ and _in spite of._ If a word shows the relation of a noun or pronoun to another word in the sentence, it's a preposition.

> A balanced diet is a cookie <u>in</u> each hand.

A **prepositional phrase** consists of the preposition plus its object and any modifiers of the object.

> The only time the world beats a path <u>to my door</u> is when I'm <u>in the bathroom</u>.

Perhaps no other rule of grammar has prompted so many to say so much as the now-outdated rule prohibiting ending a sentence with a preposition.

> *The grammar has a rule absurd*
> *Which I would call an outworn myth:*
> *A preposition is a word*
> *You mustn't end a sentence with.*
> —Berton Braley

It is, indeed, an outworn myth.

Interjection: *interj.*, a word or phrase that conveys strong emotion or surprise; an exclamation.

> Heavens, Maude!　Help!　Never!　Oops!　Cool!

The Elements of a Sentence

When the parts of speech are used in a sentence, we give them new names: subject, predicate, object, complement, and modifier.

Subject: Who or what the sentence is about.

If you put *Who?* or *What?* in front of a verb, your answer is the subject.

> _An investment in knowledge_ always pays the best interest.—Benjamin Franklin

What pays the best interest? An investment in knowledge.

A **simple subject** does not include any modifiers.

> A _conscience_ is what hurts when all your other parts feel good.

A **complete subject** is the simple subject plus all the words that modify it.

> _Constant dripping_ hollows out a stone.—Lucretius

> _Someone who thinks logically_ provides a nice contrast to the real world.

> _The best part of fiction in many novels_ is the notice that the characters are purely imaginary.—Franklin P. Adams

A **compound subject** is two or more simple subjects.

> _Banks and riches_ are chains of gold, but still chains. —Edmund Ruffin

> _Directors, coaches, and editors_ cannot teach you how to get there. But they can put you on the paths that lead there. —Thomas McCormack

Predicate: Everything in the sentence that isn't the subject.

A predicate explains or describes what the subject is doing.

> *A Canadian is someone who knows how to make love in a*
> subject   predicate
> *canoe.*—Pierre Berton

A **simple predicate** is synonymous with the verb.

> Bills <u>travel</u> through the mail at twice the speed of checks.

> A closed mouth <u>gathers</u> no feet.

A **complete predicate** includes verbs, objects, modifiers, and complements.

> Bills <u>travel through the mail at twice the speed of checks</u>.

> A closed mouth <u>gathers no feet</u>.

A **compound predicate** is two or more predicates with the same subject.

> *A poem <u>begins</u> in delight and <u>ends</u> in wisdom.*
> —Robert Frost

> *When we read, we <u>start</u> at the beginning and <u>continue</u> until we reach the end; when we write, we <u>start</u> in the middle and <u>fight</u> our way out.*—Vickie Karp

A subject or predicate is said to be *understood* if it is not actually stated but is clearly implied.

> <u>Eat</u> well, <u>stay</u> fit, <u>die</u> anyway. (The understood subject is **you**.)

Object: (1) A noun that receives or is affected by the action of the verb; (2) the noun following a preposition.

I would certainly go to the <u>barricades</u> for any <u>movement</u> that wants to sweep away the <u>Pentagon, Time magazine</u>, and <u>frozen french-fried potatoes</u>.—Gore Vidal

Barricades is the object of the preposition *to*, and *movement* is the object of the preposition *for*. *Pentagon*, Time *magazine*, and *frozen french-fried potatoes* are objects of the verb *sweep*.

A **direct object** answers the question *What?* or *Whom?* after the verb.

I hit the <u>wall</u>.	I greeted <u>Analisa</u>.
direct obj.	direct obj.

An **indirect object** receives the direct object.

I gave <u>Analisa</u> a <u>hug</u>.
    indirect   direct
    obj.   obj.

Complement: A word or phrase that completes the meaning of the verb.

Make <u>my day</u>.

Clem and Maude are learning to dance <u>the tango</u>.

Genius is <u>one percent inspiration and ninety-nine percent perspiration</u>.—Thomas A. Edison

Too many pieces finish <u>long after the end</u>.—Igor Stravinsky

Modifier: Words that describe or limit other words (see Adjective, Adverb).

<u>apple</u> pie   <u>friendly</u> advice   <u>printed</u> statement

The most successful politician is he *who says what everybody is thinking most often and in the loudest voice*.
—Theodore Roosevelt

Be careful not to misplace modifiers (see p. 39) or let them dangle (see p. 40).

Putting the Pieces Together

Sentences are made up of phrases and clauses. A **phrase** has no subject or predicate; it can serve as different parts of speech.

Prepositional phrase: under the gun

Gerund phrase: knowing the answer

Noun phrase: a nation of more than five million people

A **clause** has a subject and predicate. Clauses that express a complete thought are called **independent**; they can stand alone. Clauses that do not express a complete thought are called **dependent**; they cannot stand alone.

By the time you can make ends meet, they move the ends.
      dependent clause   independent clause

What makes a sentence a **sentence**? A subject, a predicate, and a complete thought. Anything short of a complete thought is a **fragment.**

Fragment: While I was looking at the sunset.

Complete Sentence: While I was looking at the sunset, I drove into a tree.

Used wisely, a fragment is an effective device. It provides emphasis, answers a question, or introduces a change of pace.

However, the reader should never feel that something is missing or that you just tacked on an afterthought.

A **simple sentence** consists of an independent clause.

> *Justice delayed is justice denied.*—William Gladstone

> *Too much of a good thing can be wonderful.*—Mae West

A **compound sentence** consists of two or more independent clauses; they are joined by a coordinating conjunction or a semicolon.

> *A little learning is a dangerous thing, but a lot of ignorance is just as bad.*—Bob Edwards

> *I was thirty-two when I started cooking; up until then, I just ate.*—Julia Child

A **complex sentence** consists of a dependent and an independent clause.

> *Even if you're on the right track, you'll get run over if you*
> dependent clause   independent clause
> *just sit there.*—Will Rogers

There are four more ways to classify sentences.

- DECLARATIVE: Makes a statement

  Nothing so denies a person liberty as the total absence of money.—John Kenneth Galbraith

- INTERROGATIVE: Asks a question

  Was it Frank Lloyd Wright who described television as chewing gum for the eyes?

If I counted the pages I've torn up, of how many volumes am I the author?—Colette

- IMPERATIVE: Gives an order or makes a request

  Put all your eggs in one basket—and watch that basket!
  —Mark Twain

  Fill what's empty. Empty what's full. Scratch where it itches.—Alice Roosevelt Longworth

- EXCLAMATORY: Expresses a strong emotion

  Dear God, I pray for patience. And I want it right now!
  —Oren Arnold

More About Verbs

Verbs have different forms. By changing the form of a verb, you provide the following information:

- Number
- Person
- Voice
- Tense
- Mood

Number shows if a word is *singular* (only one of something) or *plural* (more than one).

  she waltzes, he waltzes, *but* they waltz (*not* they waltzes)

Person tells who is the speaker (first person), who is spoken to (second person), and who is spoken about (third person). Person determines which verb and pronoun to use.

Voice shows whether the subject of the verb is acting (**active voice**) or being acted upon (**passive voice**).

Active voice: Celeste is assembling a computer.

Passive voice: The computer is being assembled by Celeste.

Tense tells when an action is happening: in the present (now), in the future, or in the past. As you can see in the table below, sometimes the main verb uses a helping verb to show tense.

SINGULAR	PRESENT	PAST	FUTURE
1st *Person*	I dance	I danced	I will dance
2nd *Person*	you dance	you danced	you will dance
3rd *Person*	he, she, it dances	he, she, it danced	he, she, it will dance

PLURAL	PRESENT	PAST	FUTURE
1st *Person*	we dance	we danced	we will dance
2nd *Person*	you dance	you danced	you will dance
3rd *Person*	they dance	they danced	they will dance

Mood can be considered as verbs with an attitude. Is the attitude matter-of-fact, commanding, or hypothetical? These three categories translate into the indicative, imperative, and subjunctive moods, respectively.

We use the **indicative mood** for statements of fact or questions about facts (*The dish ran away with the spoon*). We use the **imperative mood** to give commands (*Listen to me*) and to present instructions *(Place the petri dish in the sterilizer)*. Most writing is in the indicative or imperative, and using these moods is pretty automatic. But you may need a little guidance with the subjunctive.

The **subjunctive mood** conveys situations that are hypothetical, doubtful, or even contrary to fact *(If it were true…)*. Like the woman who was surprised to learn she had been speaking prose all her life, you may be unaware that you've been using the subjunctive every time you say "I wish I were rich."(For most of us, that's a condition contrary to fact.)

The New York Public Library Writer's Guide has a helpful description of the subjunctive.

> The subjunctive mood can seem like speaking English in a slightly different universe, where the basic rules of tense are reversed: Present tense is used for past, past is used for present, and *be* is used for *is, am,* and *are.*

The following examples illustrate where and how to use the subjunctive.

- An improbable condition or one that is contrary to fact

  If I <u>were</u> you, I wouldn't jump out of that airplane.

  If pregnancy <u>were</u> a book, they would cut the last two chapters.—Nora Ephron

  He spoke of his idea as if it <u>were</u> a complete solution.

- An indirect command

  The postal clerk insisted that the return address <u>be</u> included.

His piano teacher suggested that he <u>practice</u> more often.

- Motions and resolutions

  I move that the meeting <u>be</u> adjourned.

  Resolved, that my birthday <u>be</u> declared a national holiday.

Verb Forms (Verbals)

When verbs act like nouns, adjectives, or adverbs, they are called **infinitives, gerunds,** and **participles.**

Infinitives combine a verb and the word *to* (*to write, to speak*). Infinitives can act as adverbs, adjectives, or nouns.

As an adverb: I struggled <u>to fly</u> despite the strong winds.

The infinitive *to fly* modifies the verb *struggled*.

As a noun: <u>To fly</u> to Honolulu is my dream.

The infinitive *to fly* is the subject of the verb *is*.

As an adjective: For a real thrill, the place <u>to fly</u> is Rio de Janeiro.

The infinitive *to fly* modifies the noun *place*.

You create a **split infinitive** when you put a word between the verb and *to*, as in *to steadily increase* or *to boldly go*. Split infinitives have a long history of being acceptable and only a brief interlude of being frowned upon. Today, language authorities agree: If a split infinitive improves readability, split away.

We expect the advantages to more than compensate for the cost.

Gerunds are verbs that end in *-ing* and perform the job of nouns.

> <u>Playing</u> bridge <u>takes</u> concentration.
> gerund   verb

The main verb in this sentence is *takes*, not *playing*. The gerund *playing* is part of the complete subject: *playing bridge*. As a subject, it is doing the job of a noun.

> *<u>Thinking</u> is the hardest work there is, which is probably why so few people do it.*—Henry Ford
>
> *I don't think <u>living</u> in cellars and <u>starving</u> is any better for an artist than it is for anybody else.*—Katherine Anne Porter
>
> *Imagine <u>straddling</u> the cosmos, <u>clinging</u> to the tails of comets, <u>knowing</u> that time does not exist.*—Erica Jong

Participles are forms of the verb that either serve as an adjective or show tense.

- Participles acting as adjectives end in *ing, en, d, ed,* or *t.*

  swoll<u>en</u> toe   burn<u>ing</u> question   miss<u>ed</u> opportunity

- Participles that show tense vary according to the verb.

Regular verbs form the past tense and past participle by adding *d* or *ed* to the present tense.

Present Tense	Past Tense	Past Participle
dine	dined	dined
dream	dreamed	dreamed
invent	invented	invented

Irregular verbs change other letters or become an entirely different word in the past tense and past participle.

Present Tense	Past Tense	Past Participle
know	knew	known
shrink	shrank	shrunk
think	thought	thought

Participles need an auxiliary or helping verb to show tense.

I <u>might have</u> <u>thought</u> so.
   helping verb   participle

I am <u>thinking</u> about it.
helping participle
 verb

I <u>had</u> <u>thought</u> better of it.
helping participle
 verb

I <u>will be</u> <u>thinking</u> of them.
  helping   participle
   verb

A **participial phrase** combines a participle and its modifiers.

<u>The spaceship</u>, <u>lurching wildly</u>, <u>approached</u> the runway.
   subject   participial phrase   predicate

More About Pronouns

The five kinds of pronouns are personal, relative, indefinite, demonstrative, and interrogative. Pronouns are classified by how they are used in a sentence.

Personal pronouns replace nouns.

Singular: I, me, you, he, him, she, her, it

Plural: we, us, you, they, them

Possessive: my, mine, her, hers, his, our, ours, your, yours, their, theirs

Three elements determine which pronoun to use: case, person, and number.

Case: The cases of personal pronouns are nominative, objective, and possessive.

	NOMINATIVE CASE	OBJECTIVE CASE	POSSESSIVE CASE
1st Person	I, we	me, us	my, mine, our, ours
2nd Person	you	you	your, yours
3rd Person	he, she, it, they	him, her them, it	his, her, hers its, their, theirs

When a pronoun is the subject of a sentence, use the **nominative case.**

I write books. (*Not* Me write books.)

When a pronoun is the direct or indirect object, use the **objective case.**

Give me the book.

When a personal pronoun shows possession, use the **possessive case.** Possessive pronouns tell *who* or *what* something belongs to.

> The leather-bound book is <u>mine</u>.

Possessive pronouns can be in front of a noun (*my* toothache, *his* big toe) or stand by themselves (This cell phone is *yours*.)

Person: Person shows who is the speaker, who is spoken to, and who is spoken about. The speaker is the first person (*I, we*). The person spoken to is the second person (*you*). The person or thing spoken about is the third person (*he, she, it, they*).

Number: When the pronoun replaces one person or thing, use a singular pronoun (*I, me, you, she, he, it*). When the pronoun replaces more than one person or thing, use a plural pronoun (*we, you, they, them*).

NOTE: The pronoun *you* is both singular and plural.

Reflexive and intensive pronouns end in *–self* or *–selves* (*myself, themselves, yourself*). **Reflexive pronouns** refer back to someone or something already mentioned.

> *If I'd known I was going to live so long, I'd have taken better care of <u>myself</u>.*—Leon Eldred

Intensive pronouns show emphasis.

> I will drive there <u>myself</u>!

Don't substitute a reflexive pronoun for a personal pronoun.

Wrong: Give the money to Riley and <u>myself</u>.

Right: Give the money to Riley and <u>me</u>.

Relative pronouns connect words. The commonly used relative pronouns are *who, whom, which, that, whoever, whomever, whose,* and *what.*

> Rock journalism is people <u>who</u> can't write interviewing people <u>who</u> can't talk for people <u>who</u> can't read.
> —Frank Zappa

The most common error with relative pronouns is using *who* when it should be *whom* and vice versa. See p. 149.

Demonstrative pronouns are *this, that, these,* and *those.* They point to people or things without actually naming them.

I'll take six of <u>those</u>.

I wish I could play the piano like <u>that</u>!

Marisela didn't buy any property; <u>this</u> is no way to win Monopoly.

> Cross out every sentence until you come to one you cannot do without. <u>That</u> is your beginning.—Gary Provost

When *this, that, these,* and *those* precede a noun, they are adjectives, not pronouns: *that* book, *those* pickles.

Indefinite pronouns, as their name suggests, are rather vague. Examples are *any, all, several, few, some, each, every,* and compounds with *-body, -thing,* and *-one* (such as *no one, everyone, somebody, something, nobody, nothing*).

Whatever you have, spend less.—Samuel Johnson

Those who write clearly have readers; those who write obscurely have commentators.—Albert Camus

Interrogative pronouns ask questions: *who, whom, which, what,* and *whose.*

Politics is the science of how who gets what, when, and why.—Sidney Hellman

Isn't it nice that the people who prefer Los Angeles to San Francisco live there?—Herb Caen

Now let's apply the terms discussed here to the art of good writing.

Part Two
The Tools of Writing

I saw a man on a horse with a wooden leg.
See "Avoid Misplaced Modifiers," p. 39.

2 Grammatical Guidelines

> It's not just getting the right number of
> words, it's getting them in the right order.
> —John Cleese

For many people, grammar is about as much fun as a poke in the ear with a sharp stick. To them, grammarians are people who focus on nitpicky details just to make life miserable for students.

Actually, grammar helps put our language into a logical, orderly form. It makes subjects agree with verbs, places modifiers where they won't confuse readers (or make them laugh at you), and makes references clear. Communication is smooth when we follow rules. This chapter covers the most important ones.

If you need to brush up on terminology, start with the preceding chapter. If you are comfortable with nouns, verbs, subjects, and predicates, and if you can identify first, second, and third person, just jump right in.

Agreement
Make subject and verb agree both in person and number.

> Agreement is as pleasant in prose as it is in personal relations, and no more difficult to work for.—Jacques Barzun

Errors in agreement are among the most common mistakes writers make. The rule seems simple: A singular subject requires a singular verb; a plural subject requires a plural verb.

Singular:

Tom <u>is</u> late.
sing. sing.
subj. verb

Plural:

<u>Tom and Bill</u> <u>are</u> late.
pl. subj.   pl. verb

A subject in the first person also requires a verb in the first person: *I am* clever.

A subject in the third person requires a verb in the third person: *She is* clever.

But the rule is easier to state than to apply. It's not always clear what the subject is and whether it is singular or plural. So let's look at those two questions: how to identify the subject, and how to determine the number.

How to identify the subject: Three things can complicate your finding the subject.

- Intervening phrases

Phrases that come between subject and verb do not affect the number of the verb.

> <u>Identification</u> of these compounds <u>has</u> remained difficult.
>
> It is my <u>son</u>, not my daughters, who <u>likes</u> to bake bread.
>
> The <u>collision</u> between expanding human demands and Earth's natural limits <u>has</u> created unprecedented challenges.
>
> <u>One</u> in five public water systems <u>contains</u> toxic substances.
>
> *<u>Horse sense</u> is what a horse has that <u>keeps</u> him from betting on people.*—W. C. Fields

Mentally omit words that come between subject and verb to decide whether to use a singular or plural verb.

- Phrases and clauses as subjects

Use a singular verb if the subject is a phrase or clause.

> *What this country needs is a good 5-cent nickel.*
>   sing. subject   sing. verb
> —F. P. Adams

> *The best way to keep your friends is not to give them away.*—Wilson Mizner

> *The shelf life of the average trade book is somewhere between milk and yogurt.*—Calvin Trillin

- Inverted order of subject and verb

When the subject follows the verb, you may have to think twice about whether the verb should be singular or plural.

> Leading the list of Nobel Prize winners <u>was</u> <u>Linus Pauling</u>.
>   sing. verb   sing. subj.

> Seeking to defeat the legislation <u>were</u> <u>half a dozen senators</u>.
>   plural verb   plural subj.

First locate the subject and then you will know what the number of the verb should be (*most* of the time! ☺).

How to determine the number: Watch for five things that determine whether the subject takes a singular or plural verb.

- Compound subjects

Two or more subjects joined by a conjunction (*and, or, nor…*) and having the same verb are a **compound subject.** If the compound subject is joined by *and,* use a plural verb.

The <u>title and abstract</u> of the report <u>appear</u> on the first page.
  compound subj.   plural verb

<u>Writing a report and submitting it for review</u> are difficult tasks for the new manager.

<u>Motherhood and apple pie</u> <u>are endowed</u> with special virtues in the U.S.

If the compound subject is joined by *or, nor, either...or,* or *neither...nor,* make the verb agree with the word just preceding the verb.

Neither the address nor the <u>postmark</u> <u>was</u> legible.
                              sing.   sing.

Either <u>war</u> <u>is</u> obsolete or <u>men</u> <u>are</u>.—Buckminster Fuller

If you end up with an awkward sentence, rewrite.

Awkward: Neither he nor I am willing to compromise.

Better: He is not willing to compromise; neither am I.

EXCEPTIONS: If a compound subject is regarded as a single unit or refers to the same person or thing, use a singular verb.

<u>Bacon and eggs is</u> a standard breakfast for some people.

<u>My friend and former roommate is coming</u> for a visit.

Compound subjects preceded by *each* or *every* are singular.

<u>Every man, woman, and child is</u> given full consideration.

<u>Each chocolate truffle and pecan cluster is</u> individually wrapped.

Company names, even when they combine several units or names, are usually considered as a single entity and thus take a singular verb.

<u>Hy Skorz & Associates specializes</u> in college testing.

<u>Tanya Hyde & Company manufactures</u> leather goods.

- Collective nouns

Nouns such as *family, couple, group, majority, percent,* and *personnel* take either singular or plural verbs. If the word refers to the group as a whole, or if the idea of oneness predominates, use a singular verb.

The <u>faculty is</u> meeting tonight at seven.

The jury has arrived at its verdict.

The elderly couple was the last to arrive.

A minority may be right; a majority is always wrong.
—Henrik Ibsen

If the word refers to individuals or items within a group, use a plural verb.

The faculty have expressed differing views.

A couple of latecomers were escorted to their seats.

The trouble with the publishing business is that too many people who have half a mind to write a book do so.
—William Targ

In some cases rewriting avoids the problem.

Replace: The jury was clearly moved by the graphic evidence.

with: The jurors were clearly moved by the graphic evidence.

Some words take either singular or plural verbs, depending on how they are used.

Human rights is a sensitive issue. (singular)

Human rights are often ignored. (plural)

Use singular verbs with nouns that are plural in form but singular in meaning, such as *measles*, *checkers*, and *news*.

Measles is a preventable disease.

The news is broadcast daily.

Words ending in *-ics* (*statistics, politics, economics, athletics*) are singular if they refer to a body of knowledge and plural if they refer to particular activities or individual facts.

Statistics is a difficult subject. (singular)

The statistics show a declining birth rate. (plural)

Politics is perhaps the only profession for which no preparation is thought necessary.—Robert Louis Stevenson

 The word *number* is singular when preceded by *the* and plural when preceded by *a.*

The number of students enrolling is decreasing.

A number of stock market indicators were favorable.

- Indefinite pronouns

The following pronouns are always singular: *another, each, every, either, neither,* and *one,* as are the compound pronouns made with *any, every, some,* and *no* (*anybody, anything, anyone, nobody, nothing, no one...*).

Neither of the tax returns was completed on time.

When it is a question of money, everybody is of the same religion.—Voltaire

An expert is one who knows more and more about less and less.—Nicholas Murray Butler

Each of you is welcome to stay.

Nothing is so useless as a general maxim.—Thomas Macaulay

 When the word *each* **follows** a plural subject, it does not affect the verb, which remains plural.

The voters each have their own opinion.

The following pronouns are always plural: *both, few, many, others,* and *several.*

Many are called, but few are chosen.—Matthew 22:14

The following pronouns are either singular or plural, depending on how they are used: *all, none, any, some, more,* and *most.*

We've suffered some setbacks, but all is not lost. (singular)

The mistakes were costly, and all were avoidable. (plural)

None of the laundry was properly cleaned. (singular)

Three people were in the plane, but none were hurt. (plural)

The relative pronouns *who, which,* and *that* are singular if they have singular antecedents (the words they refer to) or plural if they have plural antecedents.

She is one of those rare individuals who follow directions.
                             pl. antecedent   pl. verb

She is the one student who follows directions.
               sing. antecedent   sing. verb

Sometimes rewriting solves the problem and trims wordiness as well.

> **Replace:** Honesty is <u>one</u> of the most important virtues that <u>is</u> discussed in the book.

> **with:** Honesty is one of the most important virtues discussed in the book.

- Expressions of time, money, and quantity

Use a singular verb with a total amount.

> Three dollars is a reasonable price.

Use a plural verb when referring to individual units.

> Two dollars were enclosed.

- Fractions

The number of the noun following a fraction determines the number of the verb.

> Three-fourths of the <u>ballots</u> <u>have</u> been counted.
>   plural   plural
>
> Three-fourths of the <u>money</u> <u>is</u> missing.
>   sing. sing.

> *Democracy is the recurrent suspicion that more than <u>half</u> of the <u>people</u> <u>are</u> right more than half of the time.*—E. B. White

Make pronoun and antecedent agree in number.

Agreement is important not only with subjects and verbs, but with pronouns and their antecedents. Both contribute to coherent writing.

The Labour <u>party</u> has nominated <u>its</u> candidate.
    sing. antecedent   sing. pronoun

The Labour and Conservative <u>parties</u> have nominated <u>their</u> candidates.

Each employee provides his or her (*not* their) own tools.

When following this rule means using masculine pronouns for both sexes, some writers choose to ignore the rule. However, you can usually avoid both grammatical error and sexism by rewriting.

Use the second person:

It's enough to drive <u>you</u> out of <u>your</u> senses.

Use a plural noun as antecedent:

The <u>employees</u> provide <u>their</u> own tools.

Parallel Construction

Parallel words, phrases, and clauses improve the flow of ideas and heighten its impact. Similarity of form helps readers recognize similarity of content or function.

We think according to nature; we speak according to rules; we act according to custom.—Francis Bacon

...government of the people, by the people, and for the people.—Abraham Lincoln

Canada has no cultural unity, no linguistic unity, no religious unity, no economic unity. All it has is unity.
—Kenneth Boulding

Express parallel thoughts in grammatically parallel ways. For example, pair a preposition with another preposition, a negative clause with a negative clause, and so on.

> *In an undeveloped country, don't drink the water; in a developed country, don't breathe the air.—Changing Times*

> *If one person says you're a donkey, don't mind. If two say so, be worried. If three say so, go buy a saddle.*
> *—Yiddish proverb*

Sometimes an additional preposition is needed to maintain parallelism.

> **Wrong:** The program is popular in minority communities as well as police officers.

> **Right:** The program is popular in minority communities as well as among police officers.

Use parallel construction in lists, outlines, or headings. If a list begins with strong verbs (a good idea, by the way), make the entire list begin with such verbs. The example below (from a brochure describing a writing course!) switches from strong active verbs to a wordy string of nouns and adjectives.

> 1. Add impact to every line
>
> 2. Explode writing myths
>
> 3. The simple techniques used to stimulate readers' interest

Change the third item to something like this:

> 3. Stimulate readers' interest

Modifiers
Avoid misplaced modifiers.

Sylvester picked up a girl in a blue jacket named Bonnie.

That's a misplaced modifier. It's everyone's favorite grammatical goof.

People with deficient metabolizing systems or children may be unjustly burdened by genetically engineered foods.

One day I decided to look up a style of music I'd been listening to in a big Merriam-Webster dictionary.

It's a 30-minute documentary on the Bay Area's housing and growth crisis produced by the Association of Bay Area Governments.

I found all those misplaced modifiers in books or magazines, where they had eluded the eye of copyeditors. If you want to avoid having blue jackets named Bonnie in your writing, keep related words together.

Here are some more misplaced modifiers.

Wrong: He told her that he wanted to marry her frequently.
Right: He frequently told her that he wanted to marry her.

Wrong: The clients were told their policy only covers procedures that are medically approved by their insurance agent.
Right: The clients were told by their insurance agent that their policy only covers medically approved procedures.

Wrong: The seminar is designed for adolescents who have been experimenting with drugs and their parents.
Right: The seminar is designed not only for adolescents who have been experimenting with drugs but for their parents as well.

As you can see in the above examples, word order is an indicator of meaning in the English language. Thus, it's important to place modifiers where they convey the intended meaning.

The delightfully descriptive **squinting modifier** seems to refer to words on either side of it.

A plan for laying off workers gradually is getting attention.

What does *gradually* refer to—the plan or the attention? To avoid confusion, place such modifiers directly **preceding** the word or phrase they modify. The intended meaning determines which of the following sentences is correct.

A plan for gradually laying off workers is getting attention.
or
A plan for laying off workers is gradually getting attention.

Avoid dangling modifiers.

A modifier "dangles" when what it modifies is missing or is misplaced in the sentence.

As the author of grammar books, my reputation demands error-free writing.

My reputation is not the author—*I* am!

Jogging across the busy street, a truck almost hit me.

The truck appears to be doing the jogging here. You can repair the sentence in a number of ways.

> Jogging across the busy street, I was almost hit by a truck.

> As I jogged across the busy street, a truck almost hit me.

Subtle danglers may slip by unnoticed.

> After standing in line for half the night, they announced that all the tickets had been sold.

> Having been in the Army, your editorial reminded me of the joys of being a raw recruit.

But some danglers are real howlers for which there's no excuse.

> At the age of five, his father died.

> Hidden in an antique seaman's chest, Aunt Keziah found the crucial document.

> Having been damaged in shipping, I returned the package.

> When dipped in butter, you can experience the lobster's rich flavor.

EXCEPTIONS: Certain modifying phrases are so useful that they are accepted as correct even though they dangle. *All things considered, strictly speaking, judging by the record, curiously, admittedly,* and *assuming you're right* are examples of this well-established idiom.

The word *hopefully* (as in *Hopefully, we will be on time*) should be just as acceptable, but it is still frowned on by some language mavens and by the *New York Times Style Guide*. You can stick with the *Times* or join the crowd of *hopefully* users. You can even skirt the whole issue, as I do, by finding another way to express yourself. (See p. 139.)

Double Negatives
In general, avoid double negatives.
Two negative words tend to cancel each other and create a positive meaning, which may not be what you have in mind.

> **Wrong:** The program is not going nowhere.

> **Right:** The program is going nowhere.

Not all double negatives are so obvious.

> **Wrong:** I couldn't scarcely believe what I heard.

> **Right:** I could scarcely believe what I heard.

Be especially careful when words other than *no* or *not* express negation.

Wrong: The absence of compassion was noticeably lacking.

Right: The lack of compassion was evident.

Note that *neither/nor* does not constitute a double negative; it is more in the spirit of a list of two negative elements.

Neither this nor that...

Avoid complicated negative constructions that burden the reader.

Poor: I couldn't see how it was not a disservice.

Better: I could see that it was a disservice.

You may, however, choose a double negative for its deliberate understatement (*The program is not without merit*), or for its humorous effect.

If people don't want to come out to the park, nobody's going to stop them.—Yogi Berra

Let's forget it never happened.—Ray Kass

Grammar-Checkers

Though spell-checkers are useful, grammar-checkers are more nuisance than help. Their limited rules fail to catch some mistakes while flagging other parts as errors when they are actually correct.

Altogether, you're better off using *Write Right!* to check your grammar.

𝟑 *Punctuation Pointers*

> *Anyone who can improve a sentence of mine by the omission or placing of a comma is looked upon as my dearest friend.*
> —George Moore

Punctuation marks guide your readers. Think of them as language traffic signals: Slow Down, Go That Way, Notice This, Detour. Misleading punctuation can interrupt the flow of ideas and distort meaning, but properly used punctuation helps readers grasp your meaning.

If you find a sentence particularly hard to punctuate, consider rewriting it; the problem may be one of style rather than punctuation. The well-written sentence almost punctuates itself.

Apostrophe '

The apostrophe has moved to the head of my list of misused punctuation marks. Not only is it sometimes omitted where it's needed, but even more often the apostrophe pops up where it doesn't belong (as in *it's conclusion*).

> **Wrong:** Who's chili is tastiest?
> **Right:** Whose chili is tastiest?

Wrong: Tomato's for Sale
Right: Tomatoes for Sale

Wrong: The cell phone is our's.
Right: The cell phone is ours.

Before using an apostrophe, stop to consider whether it fills any of the following needs: to show possession, to show contraction (omission of letters or numbers), or to form plurals of certain letters or words.

Use an apostrophe to show possession in the following cases.

• With singular nouns that don't end in s, add 's.

writer's cramp   employee's paycheck
witch's brew   nurse's uniform
someone's idea   fox's tail

This rule also applies to proper nouns.

Groucho Marx's mustache

Canada's climate is nine months winter and three months late fall.—Evan Esar

There are two schools of thought about adding 's to singular nouns that end in s. The traditional approach (Strunk and White, *The Elements of Style*) favors using 's at the end of all singular nouns including those ending in s.

the boss's decision   the witness's testimony

The modern approach (*N.Y. Public Library Writer's Guide*) is to use the apostrophe only.

the boss' decision   the witness' testimony

I guess that makes me a traditionalist, since *the boss' decision* makes me wonder how to pronounce it, and such a distraction seems undesirable. However, certain expressions ending in *s* (or an *s* sound) traditionally require the apostrophe only.

for goodness' sake   in Moses' lifetime

Rewriting is often the solution for an awkward possessive.

Awkward: Dickens's novels   a friend of mine's car

Better: the novels of Dickens   a friend's car

- With plural words that end in *s*, add only an apostrophe.

teachers' conference   employees' union
the Davises' vacation   witnesses' testimony
nurses' duties   guests' names

Psychiatry enables us to correct our faults by confessing our parents' shortcomings.—Laurence J. Peter

When forming the possessive of a plural noun, be sure to start with the correct plural.

the Joneses' guesthouse

- With plural words that do not end in *s*, add *'s*.

children's hour   women's issues   other people's business

! ! Never use an apostrophe with possessive pronouns *(its, hers, his, theirs, yours, ours, whose)*. By definition, these words are already possessive.

The next move is yours (*not* your's).

Wrong: The apostrophe seems to have a life of it's own.
Right: The apostrophe seems to have a life of its own.

Above all, remember that *it's* is a contraction for *it is* or *it has*.

It's easy to put the apostrophe in its place.

- If two or more individuals possess a single item, add 's to the last name only.

Tom and Dick's boat (one boat)

- If two or more individuals possess two or more items, add 's to each noun.

  Tom's and Dick's boats (two boats)

- With singular compound words, add 's to the end of the last word.

son-in-law's car	notary public's seal
Master-of-Ceremony's greeting	major domo's baton

- With plural compound words, use a phrase beginning with *of* to show possession.

  Awkward: the attorneys general's meeting

  Better: the meeting of the attorneys general

See p. 118 regarding formation of plural compounds.

- Use ' or 's in established idiomatic phrases even though ownership is not involved.

| two dollars' worth | a month's vacation |
| a stone's throw | today's jittery market |

five years' experience (*or* five years of experience)

Sometimes a hyphenated form is better: *a two-week vacation.*

Use an apostrophe in contractions to indicate omission of letters or numbers.

| summer of '02 | can't | he's |
| they're | you'd | sec'y |

I'm not denyin' the women are foolish: God Almighty made 'em to match the men.—George Eliot

If you think you're too small to make a difference, then you've never spent a night in bed with a mosquito.
—Anita Roddick

Contractions create a friendly, informal tone that may not be suitable in formal writing.

 If you aren't sure about a contraction, mentally reinsert the missing letters to see if it makes sense.

You're welcome to stay here. (You are...)

If, upon doing this, you uncover a grammatical error, rewrite.

Wrong: There's three reasons... (There is three reasons... Oops!)
Right: There are three reasons...

Use an apostrophe to form certain plurals.

- In abbreviations that have periods

  M.D.'s Ph.D.'s

- With letters when the addition of *s* alone would be confusing

  p's and q's
  The instructor handed out few A's.

- In words used merely as words without regard to their meaning

  Don't give me any *if's, and's,* or *but's.*

Avoid using 's in the following cases:

- With titles

  Poor: *All's Well That Ends Well's* ending
  Better: the ending of *All's Well That Ends Well*

- With abbreviations or acronyms

  Poor: NHL's rulings
  Better: NHL rulings

- With awkward possessives

Use an *of* phrase to avoid an awkward possessive.

  Poor: the Tower of London's interior
  a relative of mine's estate

  Better: the interior of the Tower of London
  the estate of a relative of mine

- With a name or title that is more descriptive than possessive

  Actors Equity   *Publishers Weekly*

But be careful! When I saw the following headline, I wondered how the employees had been "done" in the first place.

  Wrong: Stanford Employees Report Being Redone

  Better: Stanford Employees' Report Being Redone

Colon :
The colon is a mark of anticipation, as the following rules illustrate.

Use a colon in the following cases:

- To introduce a list, summary, long quotation, or final clause that explains or amplifies what precedes the colon

  People have one thing in common: They are all different.
  —Robert Zend

  That money talks, I'll not deny.
  I heard it once: It said "Goodbye."
  —Richard Armour

  When I am dead, I hope it may be said: "His sins were scarlet, but his books were read."—Hillaire Belloc

  In two words: im possible.—Samuel Goldwyn

Capitalize the first letter following the colon only if it begins a complete statement or a quotation. (See p. 96.)

- Following the words *as follows* or *the following*

  The recipe called for the following ingredients: black chanterelle mushrooms, Thai fish sauce, chipotle peppers, and golden caviar.

The concept of "as follows" may be implicit.

  In our country we have three unspeakably precious things: freedom of speech, freedom of conscience, and the prudence never to practice either.—Mark Twain

- In formal salutations

  Dear Senator Blowhard:

- With ratios

  2:1

- To indicate dialogue

  Margaret Fuller: I accept the universe.
  Thomas Carlyle: Gad! She'd better!

- To separate a title and subtitle

  Better Letters: A Handbook of Business and Personal Correspondence

! ! Do not place a colon immediately after a verb.

  Wrong: Prerequisites for the course are: two years of history, Sociology 101, and fluency in Spanish.

  Right: Prerequisites for the course are two years of history, Sociology 101, and fluency in Spanish.

Comma 9

In their search for an all-purpose rule, some writers place a comma wherever they would pause or take a breath when speaking. This heavy-breathing school of punctuation may leave readers feeling somewhat winded. On the other hand, too few commas create misunderstandings. You need to chart a course between those extremes, placing commas where they help readers grasp your meaning.

Use a comma to separate independent clauses that are joined by coordinating conjunctions.

An independent clause, also know as the main clause, makes a complete statement; the coordinating conjunctions are *and, but, or, nor, for, yet,* and *so.* (The clauses are underlined in the following examples.)

The English are not a very spiritual people, so they invented cricket to give them some idea of eternity.
—George Bernard Shaw

The writer is not the person, yet both natures are true.
—Fay Weldon

The optimist proclaims that we live in the best of all possible worlds, and the pessimist fears this is true.
—James Branch Cabell

> *Acrobats start their children on the high wire as soon as they can walk, and a writer ought to begin before he has graduated to solid food.*—Robertson Davies

Unless a comma is needed to prevent misreading, you may omit it between short, closely related clauses.

> *Keep your face to the sunshine and you cannot see the shadow.*—Helen Keller

> *I saw the angel in the marble and I just chiseled till I set him free.*—Michelangelo

> *Give a little love to a child and you get a great deal back.*—John Ruskin

> *Any fool can make a rule and every fool will follow it.*—Henry David Thoreau

If the clauses are long and contain commas, separate them with a semicolon rather than a comma.

> *If a man begins with certainties, he shall end in doubts; but if he will be content to begin with doubts, he shall end in certainties.*—Francis Bacon

Use a comma between the dependent and main clauses only when the dependent clause precedes the main clause. (Dependent clauses are incomplete statements; they are underlined in the following examples.)

> *As scarce as truth is, the supply has always been in excess of demand.*—Josh Billings

If you keep your mind sufficiently open, people will throw a lot of rubbish in it.—William A. Orton

If at first you don't succeed, don't take any more chances. —Kin Hubbard

Run-ons and comma faults are common errors. A **run-on,** as its name suggests, is two independent clauses that are not separated by punctuation or a conjunction. To correct the error, provide the separation by adding a period, semicolon, or comma.

Run-on: A good catchword can obscure analysis for 50 years it's the difference between a philosophy and a bumper sticker.

Corrected: A good catchword can obscure analysis for 50 years. It's the difference between a philosophy and a bumper sticker.

Run-on: Teamwork is not a preference it's a necessity.
Corrected: *Teamwork is not a preference, it's a necessity.*
—John Wooden

A **comma fault** is two independent clauses connected only by a comma or by a conjunctive adverb such as *however*. Correct the error by replacing the comma with a semicolon or period.

Comma fault: The trial itself was televised, however, reporters were barred from the courtroom during jury selection.
Corrected: The trial itself was televised; however, reporters were barred from the courtroom during jury selection.

Comma fault: Some sentences are too long, they should be broken up into more manageable chunks.
Corrected: Some sentences are too long. They should be broken up into more manageable chunks.

Use commas to separate three or more items in a series.

peanuts, popcorn, and potato chips

Early to rise and early to bed
Makes a man healthy, wealthy, and dead.
—Ogden Nash

Writing is just having a sheet of paper, a pen, and not
a shadow of an idea of what you're going to say.
—Francoise Sagan

Although journalists tend to omit the final comma to save space, language authorities recommend retaining the final comma to avoid confusion. In the following sentences, you can see the kind of trouble caused by omission of the final comma.

> In the tabloids, you can read about alien life forms, the woman who gave birth to 27 babies and Elvis Presley.

> The 15-member marching band, a drum major carrying the flag and 20 Girl Guides were all part of the Canada Day parade.

The elements in a series may be short independent clauses.

> *The only way to keep your health is to eat what you don't want, drink what you don't like, and do what you'd rather not.*—Mark Twain

> *Animals have these advantages over man: They have no theologians to instruct them, their funerals cost them nothing, and no one starts lawsuits over their wills.*—Voltaire

> *Always grab the reader by the throat in the first paragraph, sink your thumbs into his windpipe in the second, and hold him against the wall until the tag line.*—Paul O'Neil

> *First have something to say, second say it, third stop when you have said it, and finally give it an accurate title.*—John Shaw Billings

> *In America only the successful writer is important, in France all writers are important, in England no writer is important, and in Australia you have to explain what a writer is.*—Geoffrey Cotterell

When each element in the series is joined by conjunctions such as *and* or *or*, omit the commas.

> As soon as questions of will or decision or reason or choice of action arise, human science is at a loss.—Noam Chomsky

Use commas between consecutive adjectives that modify the same noun.

an inexpensive, worthwhile program

Both *inexpensive* and *worthwhile* modify the noun *program*.

> Conscience is a still, small voice that makes minority reports.—Franklin P. Jones

> The muse in charge of fantasy wears good, sensible shoes.—Lloyd Alexander

When the first adjective modifies not the noun alone but a combination of the second adjective and the noun, omit the comma.

average urban voter	cold roast beef
white tennis shoes	short attention span

Average modifies *urban voter*, not just *voter*; *white* modifies *tennis shoes*, and so on.

 One way to determine whether consecutive adjectives modify the same noun (*a young, energetic student*) is to insert the word *and* between the adjectives. "Young and energetic student" makes sense, but "short and attention span" doesn't. Use a comma between adjectives only if *and* would be a plausible alternative.

The phrase *an ugly, old fur coat* illustrates both where to use a comma and where to omit it. *Ugly and old* sounds right, but *old and fur coat* doesn't; hence, only *ugly* and *old* are separated by a comma.

white tennis shoes   *ugly, old fur coat*

Use commas where needed for clarity.

- To separate identical or similar words

  Whatever you're going to do, do it right.

- To provide a pause or avoid confusion

  Fashion passes, style remains.—Coco Chanel

Most of us would momentarily misread sentences such as the following, from which I removed the commas.

  If he chooses Williams can take over the program.

  Even though I was young when she told me that I understood her meaning.

  There were no frontiers left behind which one could hide.

  As the corpse went past the flies left the restaurant table in a cloud and rushed after it.—George Orwell

- To indicate omission of a word or words

  When angry, count ten before you speak; if very angry, a hundred.—Thomas Jefferson

Use commas to set off certain elements.

- Contrasting words or phrases

  Advice is judged by results, not by intentions.—Cicero

  The fool wonders, the wise man asks.—Benjamin Disraeli

  The less you write, the better it must be.—Jules Renard

A writer doesn't die of heart failure, but of typographical errors.—Isaac Bashevis Singer

The beautiful part of writing is that you don't have to get it right the first time, unlike, say, a brain surgeon.
—Robert Cormier

My objective is to show what I found, not what I was looking for.—Pablo Picasso

Make everything as simple as possible, but not simpler.
—Albert Einstein

Fiction is not photography, it's oil painting.
—Robertson Davies

- Phrases that are parenthetical, disruptive, or out of order

Pessimism, when you get used to it, is just as agreeable as optimism.—Arnold Bennett

Great blunders are often made, like large ropes, of a multitude of fibers.—Victor Hugo

Every man is, or hopes to be, an idler.—Samuel Johnson

Books, if you don't put them first, tend to sulk. They retreat into a corner and refuse to work.—Salman Rushdie

- Nonrestrictive phrases (phrases that add nonessential information)

The greatest discovery of my generation is that human beings, by changing the inner attitudes of their minds, can change the outer aspects of their lives.—William James

To knock a thing down, especially if it is cocked at an arrogant
angle, is a deep delight of the blood.—George Santayana

An appositive (an explanatory phrase immediately following
the word it explains) is often a nonrestrictive phrase.

> My mother, <u>the family historian</u>, found some startling infor-
> mation in the 1890 Census.

I have only one mother, so the appositive *the family historian* is
not needed to identify her.

> Stuart Keate, former publisher of the *Vancouver Sun*, once
> wrote that Canada is the vichyssoise of nations—cold, half-
> French, and difficult to stir.

Omit the commas if the phrase is defining (restrictive). In the
following examples, the restrictive phrases are underlined;
they define which noted economist, which form of taxation,
and so on.

> The noted economist <u>Milton Friedman</u> described inflation
> as the one form of taxation <u>that can be imposed without
> legislation</u>.

> *The conservative <u>who resists change</u> is as valuable as the
> radical <u>who proposes it</u>.*—Will and Ariel Durant

- Introductory phrases

> *Fortunately, there are those among us who have a healthy
> irreverence toward power, even as they seek it.*—Weir Reed

> *In the long run, it is the sum total of the actions of mil-
> lions of individuals that constitutes effective group
> action.*—Paul Ehrlich

- Direct address

  Reader, suppose you were an idiot. And suppose you are a member of Congress. But I repeat myself.—Mark Twain

  No, Agnes, a Bordeaux is not a house of ill-repute.
  —George Bain

I recently received a promotional letter from a magazine publisher with the following teaser on the envelope:

  Are you always the first to know Jan Venolia?

Actually, I know her rather well, but that's not what was meant. Avoid this kind of goof by putting a comma before the name of the person being addressed.

- Direct quotation

  John Ciardi said, "A dollar saved is a quarter earned."

  When asked to describe Charles DeGaulle, Winston Churchill responded, "He looks like a female llama who has just been startled in her bath."

  "Take some more tea," the March Hare said to Alice, very earnestly. "I've had nothing yet," Alice replied in an offended tone, "so I can't take more." "You mean you can't take less," said the Hatter. "It's very easy to take more than nothing."—Lewis Carroll

But commas are not needed before quoted material such as the following:

  Clever sayings abound on the Internet, such as "Artificial intelligence is no match for natural stupidity."

See p. 82 regarding other punctuation marks with quotations.

- Following the words *for example*, *that is*, and *namely*

  The evidence all pointed to one conclusion; namely, that the defendant was innocent.

The abbreviations for these phrases are based on Latin words and should also be followed by commas.

e.g. = *exempli gratia* (for example)

i.e. = *id est* (that is)

viz. = *videlicet* (namely)

The city council considered a proposal to streamline election procedures (i.e., to allow voting by mail).

- Conjunctive adverbs

Put a comma after adverbs that are functioning as conjunctions if you wish to indicate a pause. Examples of conjunctive adverbs are *however*, *therefore*, *indeed*, *thus*, and *consequently*.

  A shortage of platinum has halted production; consequently, we are unable to fill your order at this time.

! / The punctuation mark **preceding** the conjunctive adverb should be either a semicolon or a period, not a comma. (See p. 87.)

- Informal salutations

  Dear Tom,

- Dates and numbers

  Your letter of July 4, 1776, answers all my questions.

Put commas both before and after the year when a date is written in month-day-year order. If the date is written in day-month-year order, omit the commas.

  Your letter of 4 July 1776 answers all my questions.

For U.S. style, the use of a comma in a four-digit number is preferred (1,000); British and scientific styles omit the comma (1000). European style separates large numbers (five or more digits) with thin spaces rather than commas.

  European style: 1 426 396   45 204

  U.S. style: 1,426,396   45,204

Do not use commas in the following cases:

- Between subject and verb

  Wrong: Placing a comma between subject and verb, is incorrect.

  Wrong: Riding motorcycles, hang-gliding, and skydiving, were the main pastimes in her short life.

This error frequently occurs when a comma is placed following the last item in a series.

- Between modifier and the word modified, unless what intervenes is parenthetical or nonrestrictive (see p. 62)

  Wrong: a concise, readable, report

  Right: a concise, readable report

  Right: a concise, though readable, report

- Between elements of a compound predicate

  Wrong: On Friday I phoned his office, and was told he was not in.

  Right: On Friday I phoned his office and was told he was not in.

  He sows hurry and reaps indigestion.
  —Robert Louis Stevenson

- Between an independent and a dependent clause when the independent clause comes first (see p. 55)

  You never realize how short a month is until you pay alimony.—John Barrymore

  Everything is funny as long as it is happening to someone else.—Will Rogers

  You must always plant your feet firmly on the ground if you want to be able to jump up in the air.—Joan Miró

Dash ——

Years ago, all you needed to know about typing a dash was that it consisted of two hyphens, with no spaces before or after it.

Now, with the refinements of desktop publishing, you should know the difference between the four kinds of dash: the em, the en, the 2-em, and the 3-em dash. By choosing the right dash for the job, you produce copy that more closely resembles typeset material.

Use the em dash (two hyphens on a typewriter keyboard) for emphasis, to indicate an abrupt change, or with explanatory words or phrases.

> *It may be that the race is not always to the swift, nor the battle to the strong—but that is the way to bet.*
> —Damon Runyon

> *People want to know why I do this, why I write such gross stuff. I like to tell them I have the heart of a small boy—and I keep it in a jar on my desk.—Stephen King*

Use a pair of em dashes to replace parentheses.

> *Though motherhood is the most important of all the professions—requiring more knowledge than any other department in human affairs—there was no attention given to preparation for this office.—Elizabeth Cady Stanton*

Dashes used in this way may indicate sloppy writing. Can you substitute a comma, colon, or parentheses? Reserve the dash for those instances when you want a sharper break than a comma would provide or a more dramatic aside than you would achieve with parentheses.

> *Unwarranted dashes, the lazy author's when-in-doubt expedient, typify the gushy, immature, breathless style associated with adolescent's diaries.*—Claire Kehrwald Cook

Use the en dash (one hyphen on a typewriter keyboard) between inclusive numbers or dates.

1920–1930

pp. 106–7

! ! Do not use an en dash following words like *from* or *between*.

Wrong: from 1920–30
Right: from 1920 to 1930

Wrong: The document was written between 1875–1880.
Right: The document was written between 1875 and 1880.

Use the en dash with compound modifiers consisting of two or more words or a hyphenated word.

St. Paul–Minneapolis area

part-Hawaiian–part-Asian ancestry

Use the en dash to join a prefix or suffix to a compound.

post–World War I

Use the 2-em dash (four hyphens on a typewriter keyboard) to show that part of a word or name has been omitted.

Ms. S——
d——n

Use the 3-em dash (six hyphens on a typewriter keyboard) to show that an entire word has been omitted and to avoid repeating an author's name in a bibliography.

The suspects, ——— and ———, were led away shouting.

Venolia, Jan, *Better Letters*, Ten Speed Press, Berkeley, CA, 1995.
———, *Kids Write Right!*, Ten Speed Press, Berkeley, CA, 2000.
———, *Rewrite Right!*, Ten Speed Press, Berkeley, CA, 2000.

Ellipsis Points o o o

Ellipsis points are three equally spaced periods; they indicate omission of words or the trailing off of a thought at the end of a sentence.

Use ellipsis points to indicate an omission in quoted material.

In the middle of a sentence, use three periods.

The salary of the chief executive of a large corporation...is frequently a warm personal gesture by the individual to himself.— John Kenneth Galbraith

Between sentences, retain the period or other punctuation mark that ends the sentence before the omission.

The speaker may be forgiven if he becomes entangled in a hopeless sentence structure, but not so the writer....The speaker can use intonation, facial expression, and gesture to help where his language is lame, but written words lie quietly on the page.—Theodore Bernstein

Retain punctuation on either side of the ellipsis points if it helps clarify the meaning.

Virtually every important domestic change in the United States in recent years has been bottom up. From civil rights to the women's movement to tax revolt,...the public has been the leader and the leadership has been the follower.—Daniel Yankelovich

If entire paragraphs are omitted, retain the end punctuation of the paragraph preceding the omission and add three dots. Additional dots at the beginning of the next paragraph are unnecessary unless words are also omitted from the opening sentence.

Exclamation Point !

The exclamation point is included in this listing of punctuation marks not so much to suggest ways to use it as to caution against overusing it. Since exclamation points add urgency, surprise, or disbelief to a statement, a reader subjected to many of them begins to discredit the emotion and feel somewhat pummeled. Make the words themselves do the work.

The limited usefulness of exclamation points is brought home by the writing instructor who warns her students they will have only three exclamation points to use during their entire lifetime. A book reviewer reveals a similar viewpoint with his comment that "the book bristles with exclamation points." That said, here's where to use them.

Use an exclamation point in the following cases:

- Following an interjection

  Oops!   Congratulations!   Cool!

- Following an exclamatory statement

  I couldn't believe it when I heard the words "and the Oscar goes to…"!

- Following an imperative statement

  Don't do that again!

Place exclamation marks within quotation marks only when they are part of the quotation.

  We were startled to hear someone yell, "Man overboard!"

Hyphen ⌐

Whether to use a hyphen involves some individual choices. One person may write a compound as one word because that's what the dictionary advocates, while another sticks with the hyphenated form because it's easier to read. I tend to fall in the latter category.

I'll give the last word on hyphens to the editors of *Stet Again! More Tricks of the Trade for Publications People*:

> Hyphens exist primarily to avoid ambiguity and speed readers along. ...Everyone agrees it's better to use a hyphen where it's *not* needed than to leave it out where it's essential for sense.

See p. 116 for more discussion of compound words; see p. 97 for capitalization of hyphenated words.

Use a hyphen with certain prefixes:

- With *self-*, *ex-*, and *vice-*

  self-made   ex-wife   vice-chair

- To avoid doubling or tripling a letter

  semi-independent   anti-incumbent
  part-time   shell-like

- If the root word begins with a capital letter

  sub-Saharan   non-Euclidean   pre-Columbian

- To promote clarity

  un-ionized   anti-abortion   co-parenting
  co-worker   re-read   multi-ply

  Confusing: Recovering the sofa is next on my list of house-hold jobs.
  Clear: Re-covering the sofa is next on my list of household jobs.

Use a hyphen to form certain compound words.

Compound words unite two or more words, with or without a hyphen, to convey a single idea. Wherever possible, write compound words as one word (download, webmaster, turnkey, stockbroker); however, retain the hyphen in the following cases:

- In compound nouns, where needed for clarity or as an aid to pronunciation

  right-of-way   editor-in-chief
  dot-com   president-elect
  come-on   sergeant-at-arms

  Since television, the well-read are being taken over by the well-watched.—Mortimer Adler

- In titles that describe a dual function

  secretary-treasurer   soldier-statesman   CEO-Chair

but not job titles that describe a single function.

  attorney general   chief executive officer

- With improvised compounds

  know-it-all   stick-in-the-mud

  Johnny-come-lately   ne'er-do-well

  He spoke with a certain what-is-it in his voice, and I could see that if not actually disgruntled, he was far from being gruntled.—P.G. Wodehouse

  The authors adopted an I-can-laugh-at-it-now-but-it-was-no-laughing-matter-at-the-time attitude.—Theodore Bernstein

- With "suspended compounds"

  first-, second-, and third-quarter earnings

- In compound adjectives (unit modifiers) when they precede the word they modify

  off-the-record statement   well-known fact

  user-friendly software   state-of-the-art technology

  cost-of-living increase   London-based company

  It is important to possess a short-term pessimism and a long-term optimism.—Adrienne Rich

If modifiers follow the words they modify, they are no longer compound adjectives, and no hyphens are used.

The unit is well designed.

Their accounting methods are up to date.

Idiomatic usage retains the hyphen in certain compounds regardless of the order in which they appear in the sentence.

Tax-exempt bonds can be purchased.

The bonds are tax-exempt.

Be sure to hyphenate all the words that are to be linked.

10-year-old boy, *not* 10-year old boy

 If each of the adjectives could modify the noun without the other adjective, more than a single idea is involved (i.e., it is not a compound adjective), and a hyphen is not used.

a happy, healthy child
a new digital alarm clock

Helpful lists of compound words can be found in the *New York Public Library Writer's Guide*, *The Chicago Manual of Style*, and the *Style Manual* published by the U.S. Government Printing Office. A recent-edition dictionary will provide their editors' views on the status of various compound words (two words, hyphenated, one word). See p. 116 for more about compound words.

Is a misreading or alternative meaning possible when you omit a hyphen? If you mean *re-creation*, for example, you would give readers the wrong idea if you wrote *recreation*. Avoid creating confusing or unintentionally humorous phrases by adding all the necessary hyphens.

Confusing	Clear
caffeine free iced tea	caffeine-free iced tea
toxic waste disposal	toxic-waste disposal
man eating shark	man-eating shark
little used car	little-used car
old film buff	old-film buff
drive by assailant	drive-by assailant
self storage units	self-storage units
30 odd guests	30-odd guests

30 odd guests

Use a hyphen in the following cases:

- In fractions and compound numbers from 21 to 99

    three-fourths   thirty-seven

    Writing is one-third imagination, one-third experience, and one-third observation.—William Faulkner

- To combine numeral-unit adjectives

    12-inch ruler   5-cent cigar
    30-day month   100-year lifespan

- To combine an initial capital letter with a word

    T-shirt   X-rated
    U-turn   V-neck

- To divide a word at the right-hand margin

Do not hyphenate adverbs ending in -ly when combined with an adjective or participle.

Wrong: widely-held stock
       highly-regarded individual

Right: widely held stock
      highly regarded individual

See p. 97 for capitalization of hyphenated words.

Parentheses ( )

Parentheses are dropped into a sentence to enclose less important or explanatory information. They have the effect of an aside, as if you were trying to say the words behind your hand, so they are easily overused.

Use parentheses in the following cases:

- To set off explanatory or nonessential matter

  It is only in good writing that you will find how words are best used, what shades of meaning they can be made to carry, and by what devices (or lack of them) the reader is kept going smoothly or bogged down.—Jacques Barzun

- To provide or spell out an acronym

  Global oil supply is influenced by OPEC (Organization of Petroleum-Exporting Countries).

Punctuate sentences with parentheses as follows:

When the parenthetical matter is a complete statement, enclose punctuation within the parentheses.

  (Don't expect me until nightfall.)

When a parenthetical item falls in the middle or at the end of a sentence, place the necessary punctuation after the closing parenthesis.

  If I arrive late (and it's quite likely), I'll let myself in.

Do not put a comma, semicolon, or dash before an opening parenthesis.

  Wrong: When I arrive, (even if it's late), I'd appreciate a cup of soup.

Right: When I arrive (even if it's late), I'd appreciate a cup of soup.

The New York Public Library Writer's Guide suggests keeping the following distinctions in mind: Parentheses deemphasize information, dashes emphasize information, and commas indicate that the information is simply part of the sentence.

Question Mark ?

Place a question mark at the end of an interrogative sentence.

> *How do I know what I think until I see what I say?*
> —E. M. Forster

> *I love revisions. Where else in life can spilled milk be transformed into ice cream?*—Katherine Paterson

Do not place a question mark at the end of an indirect question or courteous request.

> He asked who would be writing the report.

> Will you please sign all the documents at the space provided.

Quotation Marks " "

Quotation marks are useful for setting off dialogue, quoted material, and special uses of words.

Use quotation marks to indicate a direct quotation.

Oscar Levant said of a politician, "He'll double-cross that bridge when he gets to it."

"I'm world famous," Dr. Parks said, "all over Canada."
—Mordecai Richler

Balanchine wanted to get me not to worry about making a masterpiece every time. "Just keep making ballets," he used to say, "and every once in a while one will be a masterpiece."—Jerome Robbins

Do not use quotation marks for an indirect quotation (a restatement of someone's words).

According to Robert Frost, a jury is twelve persons chosen to decide who has the better lawyer.

If a quotation consists of several paragraphs, do one of the following:

- Place a quotation mark at the beginning of each paragraph and at the end of the final paragraph.

- Indent and single-space the text, omitting the quotation marks.

Use single quotation marks to indicate a quote within a quote.

Friedrich Nietzsche said, "He who has a 'why' to live can bear almost any 'how.'"

Kin Hubbard wrote, "When a fellow says, 'It ain't the money but the principle of the thing,' it's the money."

Punctuate quoted material as follows:

- Place the comma and final period inside the quotation marks.

  When asked by an anthropologist what America was called before the white man came, a Native American said simply, "Ours."—Vine Deloria, Jr.

- Place other punctuation marks outside the quotation marks unless they are part of the material being quoted.

  She had the audacity to say "No"!

  You've heard of the three ages of man: youth, middle age, and "You're looking wonderful!"—Cardinal Spellman

  Do you watch "Nova"?

  On being told that President Coolidge had just died, Dorothy Parker asked, "How could they tell?"

Use quotation marks in the following cases:

- To set off individual words or a word or phrase that is being defined

  A mystery is a book the publisher thinks will sell better if it has "mystery" on the cover.—Donald E. Westlake

  The word "ventana" is Spanish for window.

  "Qualifying small businesses" means those with fewer than 250 employees.

  The two most beautiful words in the English language are "Check enclosed."—Dorothy Parker

- To enclose words or phrases following such terms as *entitled, the word(s), the term, marked, designated, classified, named, endorsed,* or *signed*

  The document was signed "John Hancock."

  I always wanted to write a book that ended with the word "mayonnaise."—Richard Brautigan

  A commentary on the times is that the word "honesty" is now preceded by "old-fashioned."—Larry Wolters

  Every word she writes is a lie, including "and" and "the." —Mary McCarthy (about Lillian Hellman)

- To indicate a misnomer or special meaning

  Some "antiques" would be more accurately described as junk.

  You may be sure that when a man begins to call himself a "realist," he is preparing to do something he is secretly ashamed of doing.—Sydney Harris

! ! A word of caution: There's an implicit sneer in this particular use of quotation marks. Don't overdo it. There is also the danger that you might be misunderstood. You'll find an amusing collection in the Gallery of "Misused" Quotation Marks at www.juvalamu.com/qmarks/. A few examples from the Web site:

- A list of ingredients that includes "real" bacon bits (maybe those are for vegetarians?)

- The law firm brochure that claims to maintain "honor and integrity" in the legal profession

- The sign in a market window that reads "Fresh" Fish

Presumably the person putting the quotation marks around a word like "fresh" did not intend to cast doubt on the word, but that's the effect created by this usage.

Unfortunately, new sightings of misused quotation marks are reported to the Web site regularly, so the list grows.

Do not use quotation marks to set off an expression that follows such words as *known as, called,* and *so-called* unless the expression is a misnomer or slang.

> *Most of our so-called reasoning consists in finding arguments for going on believing as we already do.*
> —James Harvey Robinson

Use quotation marks to enclose titles of parts of whole publications.

- Chapters or other divisions of a book

- Articles in a periodical

- Stories, essays, poems, and the like, in anthologies or similar collections

See p. 101 for rules regarding italicized titles.

Use quotation marks to enclose titles of songs and television and radio programs.

"Rule, Brittania"
"60 Minutes"
"A Prairie Home Companion"

Semicolon ;

The semicolon provides a stronger break than a comma, a weaker break than a period. It is a useful punctuation mark that careful writers employ to good effect.

> *It is almost always a greater pleasure to come across a semicolon than a period. ...You get a pleasant feeling of expectancy; there is more to come; read on; it will get clearer.—George R. Will*

However, not all writers feel so sanguine toward semicolons.

> *Semicolons are pretentious and overactive.... Far too often, they are used to gloss over an imprecise thought. They place two clauses in some kind of relationship to one another, but relieve the writer of saying exactly what the relationship is.—Paul Robinson*

If you decide that semicolons are a pleasure rather than pretentious, here's how to use them.

Use a semicolon in the following cases:

- Between closely related independent clauses that are not joined by a conjunction

The believer is happy; the doubter is wise.
—Hungarian proverb

Few people think more than two or three times a year; I have made an international reputation for myself by thinking once or twice a week.—George Bernard Shaw

Journalism allows readers to witness history; fiction gives its readers the opportunity to live it.—John Hersey

The semicolon gives equal weight to the clauses it joins, though each needs the other for full meaning.

- To separate long or complicated items in a series

  The lottery winners included an elderly gentleman who had never before bought a lottery ticket; a high school student hoping to use the winnings for college; and a reporter who had bought her ticket while covering corruption in the lottery system.

- Between independent clauses that are long or contain commas

  A neurotic is the man who builds a castle in the air; a psychotic is the man who lives in it; and a psychiatrist is the man who collects the rent.—Lord Webb-Johnson

- Between explanatory phrases that are introduced by such words as *for example, that is,* or *namely*

  The students are preparing sophisticated entries for next week's Science Fair; for example, one electronics whiz is building a virtual-reality robot.

- To separate independent clauses when they are linked by such conjunctive adverbs as *however*, *thus*, *accordingly*, *indeed*, and *therefore*

PROJECTIONS WERE GLOOMY HOWEVER, SALES SKYROCKETED.

Wrong: The coach will be late for the award ceremony, however, he does plan to attend.

Right: The coach will be late for the award ceremony; however, he does plan to attend.

Slash /

The slash is also known as the virgule, diagonal, and slant. Although it appears in informal writing more frequently now than when *Write Right!* was first published, it has limited use in formal writing.

Use the slash as a stand-in for a word or words.

- For the word *to*

  price/earnings ratio

- For the word *per*

  100 miles/hour

- For the word *or*

  and/or   his/her

- For the word *and*

  the July/August issue

- To shorten a popular expression

  24/7 (24 hours a day, 7 days a week)

However, not all of these uses of the slash can be justified. *And/or* smacks of legalese and may leave readers puzzled as to whether the slash replaces *and* or *or*. End the confusion by using one or the other. I find *he/she* hard to read, and *s/he* even more so. To avoid gender bias, use the alternatives suggested on page 37.

Occasionally, the slash indicates that the writer didn't take the time to think clearly and just cobbled together a couple of words for the reader to sort out. If a slash represents sloppy writing, rewrite.

Poor: The actress met with me to promote her movie and to dispel/explain her tumultuous offscreen image.

Better: The actress met with me to promote her movie and to dispel some of the myths behind her offscreen image.

My favorite commentary on the slash was written by Don Hauptman; it first appeared in the *New York Times* and has been widely reprinted.

Gender/Gap

The neutral pronoun "he (slash) she"
    has come into its glory.
In conversations, though, some say,
    it tends to sound quite gory.

The British, in their wisdom, call
    the "/" an oblique stroke,
Which offers a solution for
    the language as it's spoke.

To dodge offensive references
    say "he (oblique stroke) she,"
So no one claims that you endorse
    such gross misogyny.

For surely here's a case in which
    we each react uniquely.
Faced with a choice, would you opt to
    be slashed—or stroked obliquely?

Whether you call it oblique stroke or slash, I still don't like *he/she*.

4 Copyediting Considerations

If you get the form of things right,
every peril can be tamed.
—Dick Francis

Publishers and large companies often have an in-house style guide to insure uniform handling of such matters as abbreviations, capitalization, and treatment of numbers. But if you're on your own, the following guidelines will help.

When acceptable usage is a matter of personal preference, consistency is the primary consideration. Make a style sheet to keep track of which words you've capitalized, how you treated numbers or compound words, and so on (see illustration on p. 92). Refer to it when you encounter a copyediting choice to see how you handled it previously. Consistency in these matters helps readers concentrate on the subject matter.

STYLE SHEET

A B C D

dialogue	53
bi-lingual	106
bodacious	12
Breathalyzer	46
ad hominem	13

E F G H

Federalism	72, 79
eminence grise	51
halftone	43
freelance	103-5, 110
European Common Market	79

I J K L M

middle-class junkies	66
machismo	67
lowercase	21, 23, 85

N O P Q

question-begging generalization	25
the Pentagon	89
Op-Ed page	66
palimony	67, 69

R S T U V

under way	153
renege	94
right-to-die movement	123
uppercase	21, 23, 86

W X Y Z

white-collar crime	15
win-win situation	12
X-rated films	34

NUMBERS

the 20's	12

ACRONYMS, ABBREVIATIONS

OPEC	34-7
IRA	59

Abbreviations

The term *abbreviation* loosely covers three different condensed forms. An **acronym** is formed from first letters or parts of words and is pronounced as a word (NASA, OPEC). An **initialism** consists of the first letters of words and is pronounced letter by letter (SUV, NGO). An **abbreviation** is a shortened version of a word or phrase (Dept., Sec'y.).

Abbreviations take up less space and speed readers along—if they are in familiar territory. However, what is suitable for one audience may be inappropriate for another. Be aware of how much to expect of your readers. For example, the word *versus* is abbreviated as *v.* in legal citations, as *vs.* in headlines, and written out in text.

A few shortened forms have become words, their origins as acronyms all but forgotten (laser, modem, radar). Some words always appear in abbreviated form (COD, Mr., A.D., p.m.). Unless the shortened form is widely known, however, use the full name the first time it appears, followed in parentheses by the acronym or abbreviation you will use thereafter.

Choosing the correct article *(a or an)* to precede an acronym or initialism is important. Acronyms follow the usual rule for consonants and vowels: *a* precedes a consonant (a LAN user), *an* precedes a vowel (an OPEC meeting). But with initialisms, how the initial letter is pronounced determines which article to use. Certain consonants (F, H, L, M, N, R, S, and X) sound as if they begin with a vowel (*f* is pronounced "ef," *r* is "ahr," and so on). If an initialism begins with one of these consonants, *an* is the correct article (an SUV, an NGO).

Abbreviate addresses as follows:

- In an outside address (the address on the envelope), use the postal abbreviation of two capital letters and no period for a state or province. For example, write New York as NY (not N.Y.) and Quebec as PQ.

- Do not abbreviate streets or states in the inside address (the address typed on the first page of a letter). Although this rule is often ignored, observing it gives letters a more elegant appearance.

- Abbreviate compass points that follow street names.

  Porter Street NW   *or*   Porter Street, NW

- Spell out compass points that precede street names.

  1500 South H Street
  One North Broadway

Abbreviate social titles.

Ms. is now an accepted title, comparable to Mr. Use Ms. in both business and social contexts unless you know that an individual prefers Miss or Mrs.

The formal plural of the abbreviation Mr. is Messrs. and of Mrs. is Mmes. Abbreviate other titles only with the person's full name.

  Gen. George S. Patton
  Rev. Thomas Carlyle
  Gov. Peter Stuyvesant

If the full name is not used, do not abbreviate the title

General Patton, *not* Gen. Patton

In general, abbreviate dates only in informal writing.

Feb. 14, 2010   14 Feb. 2010

With partial dates and in formal usage, write dates in full.

February 14, *not* Feb. 14
14 February, *not* 14 Feb.

Use 's to form the plural of an abbreviation that has periods.

Seventy-three M.D.'s attended the meeting.

Abbreviate the following:

- *United States* and *United Kingdom* only when used as adjectives

  U.S. ambassador   U.K. foreign policy

Write out *United States* or *United Kingdom* when used as nouns.

The United States was represented by Vice President Martinez.

The United Kingdom has resisted converting to Eurodollars.

- The word *figure* only in a caption or parenthetical reference

  (fig. 1)

Capitalization

Some people have the lazy habit of writing with all capital letters. But text written entirely in capitals is hard to read. Your job is to make the reader's job easier, not harder. What's more, emphasis is lost when everything is emphasized. Which of the following gets the idea across better?

I SAID NO!   *or*   I said NO!

The following rules will help you decide when to use capital letters.

Capitalize the first word of a sentence.

Humor is the shortest distance between two people.
—Victor Borge

The only exception to this rule is when the first word is a proper noun that begins with a lowercase letter (dePriest, von Braun, eNet). If possible, rewrite so that the problem noun no longer begins the sentence.

Capitalize the first word of a complete sentence following a colon.

The company has a new policy: Every employee has three weeks of paid vacation.

Caution: Radioactive material

Do not capitalize the word following a colon if it begins an incomplete statement.

The company has a new policy: three weeks of paid vacation.

Capitalize titles as follows:

- In titles of books, plays, television programs, and so on, capitalize the first and last words, plus all principal words. Do not capitalize articles or conjunctions. Capitalize prepositions if they consist of four or more letters, or if they are connected with a preceding verb.

  Stop the World, I Want to Get Off
  Customers Held Up by Gunmen
  Situation Calls for Action
  Peace Through Negotiation

- Capitalize both parts of a hyphenated word in a title or headline unless it is considered as one word or is a compound numeral.

  Well-Known Actor Dies
  Anti-inflation Measures Taken
  Report of the Ninety-fifth Congressional District
  Son-in-law's Plea

- Capitalize personal titles only if they precede the name and are not separated by a comma.

  Professor Reynolds
  the treasurer, Will Peterson
  Prime Minister Montgomery

Capitalize the following:

- Both full and shortened names of government agencies, bureaus, departments, or services

California Dept. of Corporations   *or*   Dept. of Corporations
Bureau of Pension Advocates
U.S. Treasury Department, or Treasury Department
Library of Congress
Law Reform Commission
Board of Supervisors
Home Office
Justice Department

Do not capitalize such words as *government, federal,* and *administration* except when part of the title of a specific entity.

The U.S. Government is the largest employer in the nation.

She hopes to work for the federal government.

- Points of the compass and regional terms when they refer to specific sections or when they are part of a precise descriptive title

the East	Eastern Europe
the Southern Hemisphere	Vancouver's West End
Mid-Atlantic states	North Pole
the Orient	the Outback
Asia	the Left Bank

Do not capitalize these terms when they are suggesting direction or position.

central states	western provinces	south of town
northern lights	eastern Australia	coastal districts

Go west, young man.—John B.L. Soule

- Proper names but not descriptive words preceding them

  city of Toronto, *not* City of Toronto
  state of Vermont, *not* State of Vermont

- Abbreviations if the words they stand for are capitalized

  M.D.   Ph.D.   M.P.   J.D.   Jr.   a.m.   p.m.

- Ethnic groups, factions, alliances, and political parties but
  not the word *party* unless it is part of the name

  The Green Party is growing worldwide.

  The Democratic party will be the first to hold its convention.

  He spoke for the Korean community.

Use lowercase for political groupings other than parties.

  She represents the centrist faction of the Newspaper Guild.

  the left wing   the right wing   *but*
  the Left   the Radical Right

Capitalize *African American*, *Caucasian*, *Hispanic*, and *Native American*, but not *blacks*, *whites*, and slang words for the races.

> With white writers there are a lot of gray areas. There are commercial writers, literary writers, genre writers. But if it's black and it holds a pencil—that's the category.
> —Wanda Coleman

Problems connected with designation of the races extend beyond questions of capitalization, however. Should you use *Native American* or *American Indian*, *African American* or *black*? Styles in ethnic terminology come and go, and not everyone agrees on any given term. Your best bet is probably to choose the term used by prominent individuals in the particular group.

- Captions and legends according to individual preference or in-house style

  Please refer to figure 5.

  The chart below shows wages by skill level (fig. 5).

In general, use lowercase for the words *figure*, *table*, and *plate* and their abbreviations when they appear in text. Capitalize these terms when they appear in captions.

  Fig. 5—Wages by Skill Level

Do not capitalize the seasons.

  We always look forward to the fall colors.

Italics

Having italic type is one of the joys of word processors. When used correctly, italics enhance the appearance of any document. If you don't have italic type, use underlining.

Use italic type in the following cases:

- Titles of whole works, such as books, magazines, newspapers, movies, plays, and reports

  Granta   *Romeo and Juliet*

  Washington Post   *Gone with the Wind*

  The Hite Report   *Harry Potter and the Sorcerer's Stone*

Do not italicize the word *the* in the name of a newspaper unless it is part of the name.

> Does the library subscribe to the *Washington Post* or *The Cleveland Plain Dealer?*

Use roman type and quotation marks for titles of articles, chapters, poems, essays, and similar short works.

> "Trees"
>
> "Self-Reliance," by Ralph Waldo Emerson
>
> Chapter 12, "The Human Use of Human Beings"

- Foreign words unless they are so widely used as to have become familiar

  > Black tie is *de rigeur* for the banquet.
  >
  > The plane was en route to Algiers when they heard the news.

- For emphasis—occasionally

  Woman was God's *second* mistake.—Friedrich Nietzsche

  The correct detail is rarely exactly what happened; the most truthful detail is what *could* have happened, or what *should* have.—John Irving

  Each time I *agree* with myself, I write an essay. When I *disagree* with myself, I know that I'm pregnant with a short story or a novel.—Amos Oz

- To avoid confusion in cases where words are referred to as words, numbers as numbers, and letters as letters

  The word *alright* should be written as two words, *all right.*

  He wondered why the word *tongue* is feminine in so many languages.

  The *A's* should move to the front of the row, the *B's* next, and so on.

  If the word *arse* is read in a sentence, no matter how beautiful the sentence, the reader will react only to that word. —Jules Renard

- Short quotations when they stand alone, as at the beginning of a chapter

  When you get to the end of your life, be sure you're used up.—Edward Hoagland

Use roman type and quotation marks when the quotation is incorporated into text. (See p. 81.)

> As Mark Twain once said, "Put all your eggs in one basket— and watch that basket."

! / Never use both quotation marks and italics for the same material.

- Punctuation marks that immediately follow an italicized word if they are part of the italicized expression.

  Write Right! is a handy reference.

Numbers

When should you write numbers as words and when as figures? That depends on the nature of your writing. Nonetheless, certain conventions about numbers apply in all situations. Observe them to give your writing a professional polish.

Write numbers as words in the following cases:

- From 1 to 9 (in journalism, science, or business); from 1 to 99 (for literary writing)

  There's an old cowboy's trick. The herd is coming through fast and one cowboy asks another how you estimate the number of cows so quickly. The other cowboy says: "It's very easy. You just count the number of hooves and divide by four."—David Mamet

All you need is fifty lucky breaks.—Walter Matthau

- At the beginning of a sentence

Three hours a day will produce as much as a man ought to write.—Anthony Trollope

Thirty percent of Americans may write poetry, but I doubt that thirty percent read poetry, even their own.
—David Lehman

- In round numbers or decades

several thousand people
between two and three hundred employees
in her eighties   the Roaring Twenties

- In fractions standing alone or followed by *of a* or *of an*

one-fourth inch   two-thirds of a cup
two one-hundredths   one-half of an apple

I always try to write on the principle of the iceberg. There are seven-eighths of it under water for every part that shows.—Ernest Hemingway

- To clarify back-to-back modifiers

three 8-foot planks   six $^1/_2$-inch strips

Write numbers as figures in the following cases:

- For 10 and above (journalism, science, business); 100 and above (literary writing)

  My efforts to cut out 50,000 words may sometimes result in my adding 75,000.—Thomas Wolfe

- When numbers both below and above 10 refer to the same general subject

  5 of 20 employees
  from 6th to 12th grade

- When they refer to parts of a book

  Chapter 9   Figure 5
  page 75   Table 1

- With dates and times

  21st century   10 p.m.   5-year plan   January 1, 2010

- When they precede units of time, measurement, or money

  18 years old   9 o'clock *or* 9:00
  $1.50   75p
  2 x 4 inches $4 million
  ¼-inch pipe   10 yards
  3 hours 30 minutes 12 seconds

NOTE: Units of time, measurement, and money do not affect the rule determining use of figures when numbers appear elsewhere in the sentence.

Wrong: The 3 students each collected $50.

Right: The three students each collected $50.

Spelling

> *It is a pity that Chaucer, who had geneyus,*
> *was so unedicated. He's the wuss speller*
> *I know of.—Artemus Ward*

Unless you're a humorist like Artemus Ward, misspelling is not an asset. Misspelled words can mislead or confuse readers. They reflect poorly on you as a writer, suggesting carelessness elsewhere.

Spell-checkers help, but they aren't the whole solution. They don't pick up wrong words, particularly homophones (*there, their, they're*), so they are no substitute for knowing how to spell.

If you consider yourself a bad speller, take a look at one of the books on spelling listed in the bibliography. By learning a few rules (forming plurals, adding suffixes) and by memorizing a few spelling demons (*ei* and *ie* words), you can graduate from the ranks of bad spellers. Use the list of frequently misspelled words that begins on p. 173 as part of a spelling self-help program.

The most enjoyable way to improve spelling is to read good books. Notice how words look. You will absorb correct spellings indirectly, as if through your pores.

The person writing the copy for this ad
should have made use of the dictionary!

Part Three
The Craft of Writing

5 Words

This chapter is about "rooting around," about finding the words you want. Ours is a living language. Anthony Hughes in *The Online English Grammar* urges us to "think of it as a writhing, many-headed, sensual, changing, and wonderful creature."

Some use that vitality to justify accepting all change. If it's what people are doing, they say, it must be right. Paul Lovinger expresses a more reasonable view in *The Penguin Dictionary of American English Usage and Style*:

> New words continually appear. Those that fill needs are generally desirable. What ought to be questioned or resisted are the watering down of distinctive words that we already have, the creation of ambiguity and fuzziness, the breakdown of grace and grammar, and irrational verbal fads.

Admittedly, some changes are useful. New words have been created (*biodiversity, morph, fax, e-mail*) and old words given new meanings *(Web site, hacker, spin)*. Rules are reevaluated, and those that serve no purpose disappear. The prohibitions against ending a sentence with a preposition or starting one with a conjunction are good examples.

But when changes "water down" the richness of our language, I resist them. If *nauseous* becomes synonymous with *nauseated*, I begin to feel a little green around the gills. When the noun *loan* crowds out the verb *lend*, we all go into debt. If I've been bitten by a black widow, I need an *antidote*, not someone telling me an amusing story *(anecdote)*.

As television gobbles up increasing chunks of the day, the auditory act of hearing replaces the visual act of reading. Along the way, nuances between words disappear, and our writing becomes peppered with malapropisms:

Wrong	Right
for all intensive purposes	to all intents and purposes
one in the same	one and the same
tongue and cheek	tongue in cheek
straightened arrow	straight and narrow

If we allow our language to be whittled down, we lose cultural information; this, in turn, reduces our ability to understand the world and our place in it. Let's use words as our vote for clarity, for felicity, for celebration.

The Prerequisite for Good Writing:
A Good Dictionary

A good dictionary is essential in searching for the right word. Among other things, you'll find an exploration of the shades of meaning that will guide your choice.

Take the words *doubtless* and *no doubt*, which my dictionary describes as follows:

> ...relatively weak in expressing certainty, since they can also indicate mere presumption or probability: "He will doubtless go"; or concession: "You are no doubt right in some details." In contrast, *undoubtedly* and *without doubt* express only certainty and conviction.

The dictionary goes on to say that *doubt* and *doubtful* are often followed by clauses beginning with *that*, *whether*, or *if*, and it recommends that I look up *doubtful*, *dubious*, and *questionable* for additional shades of meaning. Have I left any doubts that you'll find a dictionary invaluable?

 What *is* a good dictionary? If you're shopping for one, I recommend looking up a few words. If the candidate dictionary lists *heighth* without advising you that this is nonstandard usage or if it lists *irregardless* without pointing out the redundancy and suggesting that you use *regardless*, keep looking.

Here are a few of the types of information included in a dictionary:

- Usage, including levels of formality (formal, standard, slang)

- Etymology (word roots)

- Abbreviations

- Pronunciation

- Inflected forms (e.g., *well, better, best*)

- Parts of speech

- Synonyms

A thesaurus, with its everything-under-the-sun approach, expands your choice of alternative wording still further. When Dr. Roget published his first thesaurus in 1852, he said it was for "those who are...struggling with the difficulties of composition." Roget and those who followed have provided us strugglers with an abundance of words to choose from.

As an example, let's walk through the treatment of the word *walk*. It is one of the forty-three categories of entries under "Travel" in my thesaurus. A few of the alternatives included are the highbrow *ambulate*, the descriptive *stride*, the casual *hoof it*, and the quaint *ride shank's mare*. What a treasure trove of choices!

A word processor's dictionary and thesaurus are no substitute for the real thing. When I was considering the wording of the previous paragraph, I looked up *trove* in my word processor's thesaurus. The only alternative it suggested was *trowel*!

A dictionary is helpful *only if you use it*. Look up words often, and while you're there, take advantage of the wealth of information at your fingertips.

> *Develop a respect for words and a curiosity about their shades of meaning that is almost obsessive.*—William Zinsser

A Note About British and American Usage

The differences between British English and American English are beyond the scope of this book. Each has a distinct vocabulary, spelling, punctuation, and usage.

American	British
color, jewelry	colour, jewellery
trunk, elevator	boot, lift
Mr.	Mr
in the hospital	in hospital

Nonetheless, our common heritage in language is so extensive that the rules and conventions of American English presented here cover most situations. If you need more information about the differences between British and American English, look at some of the books listed in the bibliography or search the Internet (my search for "British language usage" produced more than 30,000 hits!).

> *The Americans are identical to the British in all respects except, of course, language.*
> —Oscar Wilde

Compound Words

The word *compound* means "consisting of two or more elements." Compound words unite two or more words to convey a single idea. Whether to write compounds as two words (*real estate*), hyphenated (*off-the-record*), or one word (*motherboard*) is a vexed question. Fixed rules are hard to come by.

For example, you can't make a single, all-purpose rule about compounds beginning with the word *cross* since they fall in all three categories: *crossfire, cross-country*, and *cross hair*. Let your choice be guided by whether hyphenating a compound helps the reader.

Here are a few suggestions, from the firm to the flexible, for dealing with the compound predicament.

Two-Word Compounds

Some two-word compound nouns go together so naturally that we don't need to add hyphens or make them one word for the sake of clarity. Even when such compounds are modifiers, no hyphens are needed.

Noun	Adjective
civil rights	civil rights attorney
high school	high school graduate
data processing	data processing center

One-Word Compounds

Similarly, some compounds are so well established as one word that we hardly realize they are compounds.

blackout	pickup	wallpaper
checkbook	guidelines	desktop

Others are still evolving toward the one-word form. *Multitasking* has made the transition, while *Web site* is still in the process (*Web site*, *web site*, and *website* are all currently acceptable). Once you've made a decision, stick with it. If you begin with *start-up companies*, don't switch to *startup companies* mid-document.

Some one-word compounds are formed from a verb and a preposition.

<u>shut</u> + <u>down</u> = shutdown
  verb   prep.

These are handy as nouns (*backup*, *runoff*) and as modifiers (*a backup procedure*, *runoff elections*). But you run into trouble if you use such compounds as verbs.

Wrong: Did you backup your file?

Right: Did you back up your file?

By retaining a two-word, unhyphenated verb form such as *back up*, *run off*, and *set up*, you will avoid a monstrosity like *I back-upped my files*.

Hyphenated Compounds
By hyphenating compound modifiers that precede the noun, you help readers see how the words are connected.

    pale-green soup
    teacher-training program
    part-time employee

See p. 74 for more about hyphenated compounds.

Plural Compound Words

Form plurals of compound words with the principal word.

notaries public   mothers-in-law
attorneys general   major generals
deputy chiefs of staff   commanders in chief
passersby   courts-martial

Medium-size or Medium-sized Business?

The language submits to no rules when it comes to this kind of decision. Certain *-ed* forms are well established.

left-handed pitcher   four-legged animal
two-pronged approach   long-stemmed glasses

But is it *bite-size pieces* or *bite-sized pieces, horn-rim glasses* or *horn-rimmed glasses, teenage boy* or *teenaged boy*? In *The Careful Writer*, Bernstein concludes that it's a matter of "idiom and sound." In other words, use the form that sounds right to you.

> *You can scrutinize whole categories of words and sometimes imagine you have hit upon a principle, but as soon as you do, the next word you can think of constitutes an exception.*—Theodore Bernstein

Trendy Words and Clichés

> Ready-made phrases are the prefabricated
> strips of words...that come crowding in
> when you do not want to take the trouble
> to think through what you are saying.
> —George Orwell

The saturation provided by television, radio, and the various print media can turn words into instant clichés. *Paradigm, viable options, closure, epiphany, no problem, déjà vu, bottom line, 24/7, basically, radar screen, behind the curve, killer app,* and *rocket scientist* have all joined the catalog of overworked words. A good *news/bad news* format may have been fresh once, but it has lost its edge.

The best way to stifle word fads is to ignore them. Allow the overworked expression to recuperate.

> My inclination is to question deviant forms,
> challenge innovations to prove themselves,
> and resist senseless fads.—Paul Lovinger

As for clichés, that's where the rubber hits the road. If you're trying to hit the nail on the head and not mince words, it goes without saying that clichés won't do the trick. They seldom throw any light on the subject and probably should never see the light of day. Are we all on the same page?

Jargon

Jargon can be useful shorthand; specialized vocabularies allow members of a professional group to communicate succinctly with each other. But jargon has earned its bad reputation because it is often used simply to impress, or worse yet, to provide a smokescreen for burying truth rather than revealing it. Examples: "revenue enhancement" for taxes and "proactive resource-allocation restructuring" for closing the factory and moving to Mexico.

Everyday jargon includes the following elements: interchangeable parts of speech and noun chains.

Interchangeable Parts of Speech

The English language is remarkably adaptable. It allows us to shuffle parts of speech around, turning nouns into adjectives (*milk carton*), verbs into nouns (*on the mend*), nouns into verbs (*to face*), and adjectives into nouns (*seeing red*). Indeed, such flexibility is one of the strengths of our language. But avoid such "verbs" as *to guest* and *to gift*.

Poor: This model obsoletes its predecessor.
Better: This model makes its predecessors obsolete.

Occasionally pressing nouns into service as verbs (or vice versa) creates a breezy style. In striving for a certain effect, I might write "Let's front-page that story." I would draw the line, however, at "I plan to Op-Ed my views in the Sunday paper" or "The investigator accessed the information in the public library." And I would quickly put aside a handbook on writing if I found a chapter titled "How to Style Written English."

Noun Chains

Nouns used as adjectives often slip out of a writer's control, producing impenetrable chains. To break these into manageable chunks, look for the noun at the end of the chain. Move it forward and turn the other chunks into short prepositional phrases.

> **Rewrite:** potassium permanganate-impregnated activated alumina medium
> **as:** a medium of activated alumina that has been impregnated with potassium permanganate

> **Rewrite:** urban public hospital out-patient clinics
> **as:** out-patient clinics sponsored by urban public hospitals

Revisions of noun chains are often longer than the original phrase. That's a price we pay for clarity. In a contest between brevity and clarity, clarity should always win.

Unintended Meanings and Other Foolishness

Pause to think about what you've written. In the heat of creation, you may fail to notice something as ridiculous as "the world's largest van for its size." Or how about a "precise estimate"? Perhaps you likened a frenzy of activity to the "eye of the storm," when in reality calm is what characterizes the eye of a storm. If you describe a point of new beginning as "ground zero," you are actually referring to the point of maximum impact (hence, maximum destruction), not to fresh ground.

> *The slovenliness of our language makes it easier for us to have foolish thoughts.*
> —George Orwell

Step back and take a fresh look to save yourself embarrassment. Those who wrote the following sentences (all of which appeared in print) failed to do that.

No job losses are planned.

Submit a list of all employees broken down by sex.

No detail is too small to overlook.

We feel pornography is an issue that demands a second look.

Dr. Ruth will talk about sex with Larry King.

(Sign in cemetery) Persons are prohibited from picking flowers from any but their own graves.

Some English words (called **homographs**) have identical spellings but different pronunciations and meanings. Take the word *subject*. When the word is a noun, the accent is on the first syllable (*súbject*) and it means a topic or an individual; when it's a verb, the second syllable is accented (*subjéct*) and it means to cause to undergo.

We had to subject the subject to a series of tests.

Be aware when using a homograph that readers may not know how to interpret a word unless the context makes it clear.

Confusing: The bandage was wound around the wound.

Better: The bandage was tightly wound around the wound.

Better yet: The wound was tightly bandaged.

Tricky Words

English is riddled not only with homographs, but also with homonyms and homophones. **Homonyms** are words that are both spelled and pronounced alike: *bear* the animal and *bear* the verb. **Homophones** are words that have different spellings but the same pronunciation: *write* and *right*. Some words have similar sounds (*home/hone*), and others call for a specific usage (*myriad details*, not *a myriad of details*). No wonder we have trouble!

The following words seem to invite error. Skim through the list to see if it includes words you use and if you're using them correctly. Refer to the list as needed to help you find just the right word and its correct use.

The status of some entries listed below is changing from unacceptable to widely accepted in formal writing. During the transition, careful writers will continue to observe the traditional usage.

Advice, Advise: The noun *advice* means a suggestion or opinion concerning a course of action. The verb *advise* means to give advice; using *advise* as a synonym for *inform* smacks of business jargon. Someone who dispenses advice is either an *adviser* or an *advisor*; both spellings are acceptable, but *adviser* seems to have the edge.

Affect, Effect: *Affect* is most often used as a verb and *effect* as a noun. The verb *affect* means to influence or to have an effect on.

> The attorney hopes to affect the jury's decision.

A less common meaning of *affect* as a verb is to pretend in order to make a desired impression.

> The prosecutor affected a look of amazement when the defendant couldn't recall his whereabouts.

The noun *effect* means result or consequence.

> The effect of the program change was to reduce overtime.

The verb *effect* means to bring about.

> Management hopes to effect a similar change in employee benefits.

Aggravate: A verb meaning to make worse. A trouble or condition is aggravated, not a person.

> The condition of the road was aggravated by the flooding creek. Esmeralda was provoked (*or* annoyed *or* irritated) when she couldn't reach her mailbox to see if she had won the sweepstakes.

All- (all right, almost, already, altogether): Three of these have both one- and two-word forms, each with its own spelling and meaning. One, *all right*, is correct only in the two-word form; *alright* is a misspelling of *all right*.

The literal meaning of *all right* is entirely right, and its less formal meanings are adequate, permissible, and satisfactory. *Almost* means not quite. *Already* means by this (or a specified) time. *Altogether* means entirely or on the whole.

The two-word forms of these words have different meanings, which you can deduce from the following examples. Failure to note the differences could be embarrassing, as the first example illustrates.

> The cookies and pies are almost baked; you are all most welcome to join us for dinner.

> By the time we were all ready, the plane was already taxiing to the runway.

> They were not altogether happy at being all together again.

Allude, Elude, Refer: To *allude* to something is to mention it indirectly, without identifying it specifically. To *refer* is to indicate directly.

> The speaker alluded to the hazards of smoking when he referred to the chart showing the incidence of lung cancer.

Elude means to slip away from or avoid.

> The suspect managed to elude the police.

Alternate, Alternative: The strict meaning of *alternate* as an adjective refers to every other one, or succeeding by turns: *alternate* days means every other day. It is now more loosely used to mean offering a substitute (*an alternate route*). As a

Alternate   Alternative

noun, *alternate* means a substitute (*an alternate at the convention*). *Alternative* as a noun means a choice (*an alternative to war*). As an adjective, *alternative* has strayed from its strict meaning of one of two choices to mean simply providing a choice (*an alternative plan*).

Ante-, Anti-: *Ante* means coming before or in front of.

antebellum = before the war
antediluvian = before the floods

Anti means against.

antifreeze   anti-establishment

Just to confuse matters, *anti* is also a variant of *ante* in such words as *antipasto*, where it means "before the first course."

> His fondness for latte and antipasto antedates their widespread popularity.

Anticipate: A verb meaning to take action beforehand. Described by Paul Lovinger as a "wounded word," *anticipate* should be used only in this sense, not as a synonym for *expect*.

> The chess master anticipated his opponent's every move.

Anxious, Eager: Use *anxious* where there is a sense of anxiety, *eager* where there is pleasant expectation.

The grandmother awaited the birth of her first grandchild anxiously; she was eager to hold the baby in her arms.

Apt, Liable, Likely, Prone: *Apt* implies a natural tendency (*I am apt to forget their names*). *Liable* suggests the possibility or probability of risk (*The theme of the ad campaign is liable to be misunderstood*). *Likely* conveys simple probability (*The forecast says rain is likely*). *Prone* means tending (*People who are accident-prone have a tendency to fall often or to cut themselves with sharp knives.*)

A While, Awhile: *While* means a period of time; *awhile* means *for* a period of time. Thus, to write "I will be gone for awhile" is to double up on the word *for*. Write "I will be gone for a while" or "I will be gone awhile."

Bad, Badly: To help you decide which of these two words to use, substitute another adjective or adverb for *bad* or *badly* in the sentence. For example, in the sentence "I feel bad (or badly) about the results," substitute the adjective *unhappy* and the adverb *unhappily*.

I feel unhappy/unhappily about the results.

Clearly, you wouldn't write "I feel unhappily"; therefore, choose the adjective and write "I feel bad."

Beside, Besides: When you mean "next to," use *beside*; when you mean "in addition to" or "except for," use *besides*.

Besides the defense attorney, no one was willing to sit beside the prisoner.

Better/Best; Worse/Worst: When you're comparing the merits of two things or people, use *better* (or *worse*); when comparing three or more, use *best* (or *worst*).

Between, Among: An ill-founded rule calls for using *between* with two items and *among* with more than two. Doggedly following this rule can lead you into such an absurdity as *She traveled among Santa Fe, Taos, and Albuquerque.* A better rule is to use *between* when individual relationships are emphasized and the number is unspecified (*he appeared between acts; cooperation between neighboring countries*), and when repetition is implied (*sobbing between breaths*). Use *among* with unspecified numbers if individual relationships are not emphasized (*discontent among the employees*). You are probably on safe ground using whichever word sounds right. The following examples illustrate choices that sound right.

The anthropologist traveled among the Navajo and Hopi.

She traveled between Rome, Paris, and Berlin.

Watch out for illogical constructions that include the word *each* or *every: He was sobbing between each breath.*

Bi-, Semi-: If you want to avoid confusion when referring to a period of time, consider abandoning the use of the prefixes *bi* and *semi* and say every two weeks, every two months, twice a year—or whatever interval you are describing.

Billion: Means a thousand million (1,000,000,000) in the United States but a million million (1,000,000,000,000) in the United Kingdom. Where appropriate for your audience, specify which meaning you're using.

> three billion (U.S.)
> 1.5 billion (U.K.)

Can, May: The rule that distinguishes between *can* (the ability or power to do something) and *may* (permission to do it) is weakening. The *Harper Dictionary of Contemporary Usage* considers this "rather a pity, for the distinction is a nice one—and not really very hard to remember." Formal usage still requires the use of *may* for permission, despite the prevalence of *can* for *may* in speech.

Capital, Capitol: *Capital* refers to wealth, the city that is the seat of government, or an uppercase letter. *Capitol* is the building in which state or federal officials congregate. The *Capitol*, when referring to the home of the U.S. Congress, is always capitalized.

capital
(*money*)

capitol
(*building*)

capital C
(*upper case*)

People who work in the Capitol disburse a great deal of the taxpayers' capital.

 Only <u>o</u>ne building in the U.S. is the Capit<u>o</u>l, and only <u>o</u>ne building in each state is its capit<u>o</u>l; <u>a</u>ll others are capit<u>a</u>l.

Complement, Compliment: *Complement* is both a verb and a noun, meaning to complete a whole or satisfy a need. *Compliment* also functions as both verb and noun, meaning praise.

Her efforts <u>complemented</u> those of the rest of the team.
verb

A <u>complement</u> of twelve laborers performed the task.
noun

She <u>complimented</u> him on the apple pie he had baked.
verb

Her <u>compliment</u> was sincere.
noun

Nowadays we are all of us so hard up that the only pleasant things to pay are compliments.—Oscar Wilde

Comprise: Means to include or be made up of; therefore, *comprised of* is redundant. It is frequently confused with *compose* or incorrectly used as a synonym for *constitute*. The traditional dictum is that the whole comprises the parts; the parts constitute the whole. If *comprise* sounds stilted, substitute *is composed of*.

Wrong: High-tech companies comprise only 10 percent of GNP.

Right: High-tech companies constitute only 10 percent of GNP.

Right: The company comprises three divisions.

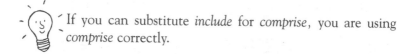 If you can substitute *include* for *comprise*, you are using *comprise* correctly.

Contact: This word seems to have made the complete transition to respectability as a verb, but I might still look for a more descriptive alternative.

Continual, Continuous: *Continual* means over and over again; *continuous* means uninterrupted or unbroken. Dictionaries now list these words as synonymous, but maintaining the distinction between them helps preserve the richness of our vocabulary.

Since he coughed continually, the doctor kept him under continuous observation.

A man's memory may almost become the art of continually varying and misrepresenting his past, according to his interests in the present.—George Santayana

Convince, Persuade: Though the meaning of these words is similar (to bring to belief), each has a preferred usage. You persuade someone to do something, but you convince someone

about something. In other words, *convince…of*, but *persuade…
to/that/as to/about*.

> He convinced me of his sincerity.

> He persuaded me that she was sincere.

> She persuaded me to attend the meeting.

Cope: Careful usage limits *cope* to coping *with* something, not
just coping.

Council, Counsel, Consul: *Council*, always a noun, refers
to an assemblage of persons or a committee. *Counsel* has both
verb and noun forms, meaning to advise, the advice itself, or
an attorney.

> Counsel for the defense counseled her client not to speak to
> the council members; the council resented her counsel.

Consul is a person in the foreign service who represents the
business interests of the country.

Cum: A recently popular way to indicate a coupling, as in
bookstore-cum-coffeeshop. As with many word fads, this one is
easily overdone.

Data: A plural Latin word meaning information, especially in
numerical form. Acceptance of *data* as a singular is widespread,
and it has all but eliminated use of the Latin singular *datum*.
However, in scientific and formal writing, the plural form is
still preferred.

> Data are… (*not* Data is…)

Decimate, Annihilate: The literal meaning of *decimate* is to destroy one-tenth of, though it is sometimes loosely used to mean to destroy a large part of. *Annihilate* means to destroy completely (thus, *annihilate completely* is redundant). The words *decimate* and *annihilate* are not interchangeable.

Different from, Different than: *Different from* is preferred in most cases, especially if it is followed by a single noun, pronoun, or short phrase.

His writing style is different from mine.

Different than is acceptable if it avoids wordiness or is followed by a clause.

Wordy: Writing style today is different from what it was a century ago.

Better: Writing style today is different than a century ago.

Dilemma, Predicament, Hobson's Choice: Reserve the use of *dilemma* for a choice between two equal alternatives; to refer to a difficult situation, use such words as *predicament, plight,* or *problem. Hobson's choice* is the apparent freedom of choice when there is no real alternative; it is named for Thomas Hobson, a seventeenth-century liveryman who gave customers the choice of the horse next to the stable door or no horse at all.

Disburse, Disperse: *Disburse* means to pay out, as from a fund; *disperse* means to scatter.

He disbursed the proceeds of the estate after he had dispersed the ashes.

Discreet, Discrete: *Discreet* describes behavior that is prudent or respectful of propriety. *Discrete* frequently has a scientific connotation and means separate, distinct, or individual.

> She made discreet inquiries into his whereabouts.

> The smooth surface of water seems to contradict the discrete nature of its molecules.

Disinterested, Uninterested: Cautious writers still observe the distinction between these two words. *Disinterested* means objective or impartial, not influenced by personal advantage. *Uninterested* means indifferent or lacking interest in an outcome.

> A disinterested scientist is not uninterested in the outcome of her experiments.

Due to, Because of: Though used interchangeably in informal writing, careful writers will use *because of* to indicate a cause-and-effect relationship and reserve *due to* for use after forms of the verb *to be*.

> The driver lost control of the car because of faulty brakes.

> The collision was due to faulty brakes.

Ecology: The study of the relationship between organisms and their environment. Often misused as a synonym for *environment*, which means surroundings.

Emigrate, Immigrate: To *emigrate* is to leave one's country permanently; thus one emigrates **from** a country. To *immigrate* is to move to a new country permanently; thus one immigrates **to** a country.

Eminent, Imminent, Emanate: *Eminent* means well known or distinguished; *imminent* means about to happen; *emanate* means to originate or issue forth.

> The arrival of the eminent statesman was imminent.

> A light emanated from the shuttered windows.

Enthused: A "back formation" from the word *enthusiasm* (as *donate* was derived from *donation*), *enthused* is not yet acceptable in formal writing. Use *enthusiastic*.

Farther, Further:

Traditional American usage calls for *farther* when actual physical distance is involved (*We walked farther than we had intended*). Use *further* in the sense of more or additional (*further deliberation, going further into debt*) and in the figurative sense of distance (*We are moving further from the truth*).

Fewer, Less: *Fewer* is used with individual items that can be counted (*fewer potatoes*); *less* is used for quantity or bulk, when the item is regarded as a single entity (*less oatmeal*).

> The fewer mistakes you make, the less embarrassment you will feel.

> A diet that has less fat will also have fewer calories.

Less takes a singular verb and *fewer* a plural one.

> Less fat is needed if fewer calories are to be consumed.

Finalize: Resistance to this word because of its bureaucratic flavor appears to be waning, perhaps because substitutes are wordy (*to put in final form*) or fail to convey the same meaning (*conclude, complete*). Nonetheless, *-ize* words such as *finalize* and *prioritize* create an inelegant patina that you might want to avoid in formal writing.

Flammable, Inflammable: Both mean capable of burning. Because of the danger that *inflammable* will be mistaken for not flammable, use *flammable* to mean combustible and *non-flammable* for its antonym.

Flaunt, Flout: A common error is to use *flaunt*, which means to show off, for *flout*, which means to show contempt. Although sometimes widespread errors evolve into acceptability, confusing these two words is simply an error.

> Even in an academic setting, he flaunted his superior knowledge.

> They tried to flout U.S. tax laws by establishing offshore accounts.

Foreword, Forward: Mixing up these two words is a serious blunder, especially in large print at the front of a book. *Foreword* is a preface or introductory note. It deals with words and is spelled with an o. *Forward* is the opposite of backward and means at or near the front, or moving in the direction of the front. There is no such word as *foreward*.

Fulsome: Modern usage limits the meaning of *fulsome* to offensively excessive or insincere; disgusting. This word is often used incorrectly to mean abundant or lavish. Don't write *fulsome praise* unless you wish to be uncomplimentary.

Gender, Sex: *Gender* is a grammatical term that classifies words as feminine, masculine, or neuter. In recent years, it has been increasingly used as a euphemism for *sex* when identifying whether a person or animal is male or female. When filling out forms nowadays, you may be asked for age, income, and gender. As Paul Lovinger says, "It is not obvious why *sex*, in such an innocent sense, needs a euphemism." But for now, it seems *gender* will be used to indicate sex and *sex* to indicate the sexual act or sexual activity.

Get, Got: Although *get* and *got* can claim a long history of use in the English language, careful writers will avoid their casual overtones by substituting words such as *have* or *receive* whenever possible.

> I've got the answer. (I have the answer.)

> We've got to comply. (We have to comply *or* We must comply.)

In some cases, *got* remains a suitable choice.

They got what they deserve.

Heighth: A non-word. The correct word is *height*.

Home, Hone: The verb *hone*, meaning to sharpen, is sometimes incorrectly substituted for *home* in the expression *home in*, meaning to be guided to a target.

> **Wrong:** He honed in on the target.

> **Right:** He honed his skills in order to earn a promotion.

> **Right:** The airplane homed in on the runway.

Homogeneous, Homogenous: *Homogeneous* means uniform in structure or composition throughout. *Homogenous* is correctly used in biology to indicate a correspondence between organs or parts that are related by common descent. However, it appears more often as a misspelling or mispronunciation of *homogeneous*.

Hopefully: This adverb means full of hope (*He uttered his prayer hopefully and fervently*). The more common usage today is in place of "I hope" (*Hopefully, I will receive a raise*). A great deal of ink has been spent trying to forestall acceptance of *hopefully* in the latter sense. But just as *happily, presumably,* and *luckily* have been accepted as standard usage, *hopefully* may someday cease to grate on the nerves of traditionalists. For now, a strong case can be made for avoiding the word simply because it is overworked. I *hope* I make myself clear!

I, Me, Myself: *I* is the subjective case and thus should be used when it is the subject of a sentence (the *who* or *what* the rest of the sentence is about).

My brother and I went to the ball game.

Me is the objective case and should be used when it is the object of the action or thought conveyed by the verb of the sentence, or when it is the object of a preposition.

Between you and me, I hate Sunday afternoon football.

Ebenezer invited Elijah and me to the opera.

In a sentence such as the last, if you remove "Elijah and," it is obvious that *me* is the correct pronoun.

Myself is correctly used for emphasis (*I, myself, will see to it*) or as a reflexive (*I hurt myself falling from the roof*). Do not use *myself* as a substitute for *I* or *me*.

Wrong: The money was given to my partner and myself.
Right: The money was given to my partner and me.

Wrong: My partner and myself are seeking underwriting for a business venture.
Right: My partner and I are seeking underwriting for a business venture.

Impact: A noun meaning violent contact, as of two objects striking each other. Do not use it as a substitute for *effect, influence*, or *result*. As a verb, it's a poor substitute for *affect*.

Imply, Infer: To *imply* is to suggest directly or insinuate; to *infer* is to draw a conclusion or deduce.

I infer from your remark that no threat was implied.

Insure, Ensure, Assure: All three words mean to make secure or certain.

Victory is assured. (*or* ensured *or* insured)

Assure has the meaning of setting someone's mind at rest. Both *ensure* and *insure* mean to make secure from harm. Only *insure* should be used regarding guaranteeing of life or property against risk.

Irregardless: A redundancy. Use *regardless*.

It's, Its: *It's* is the contraction of *it is* or *it has*. *Its* is a possessive pronoun. (See p. 48.)

Lay, Lie: *Lay* is a transitive verb (i.e., it takes an object); it means to place or put down. The past tense and past participle form is *laid*.

> Lay the package on the table. (**package** is the object of the verb **lay**)

Lie is an intransitive verb (i.e., it does not take an object); it means to recline. The past tense of *lie* is *lay*; the past participle is *lain*.

> Lie on your exercise mat.

> He lay on the mat for half an hour.

> He had lain on the mat for half an hour when I arrived.

 To help you decide whether to use *lay* or *lie*, substitute the word *place*. If *place* sounds right, use *lay*.

Lend, Loan: Call me old-fashioned, but I still prefer to distinguish between the verb *lend* and the noun *loan*. Doesn't "I will lend you my pen" seem more elegant than "I will loan you my pen"? Despite its widespread acceptance as a verb, I will continue to use *loan* only as a noun (*I received a $1,000 loan*).

Like, As: *Like* is correct when used as a preposition (in other words, when it's followed by a noun or pronoun).

> She writes like Hemingway.

> *My Luv is like a red, red rose.*—Robert Burns

Like is also acceptable when it introduces a clause from which the verb has been omitted.

> He took to politics like a fish to water.

In formal writing, substitute *as* or *as if* for *like* when it's used as a conjunction.

> Residents of the model village live <u>as</u> the villagers did two hundred years ago.

> The shareholder spoke <u>as if</u> he had privileged information.

In journalism and informal writing, *like* is often used as a conjunction.

> Sales aren't growing like they were a decade ago.

Literally: Although a *literal translation* is word for word and exact, *literally* has strayed into being used for emphasis in ways that are anything but literal. Your credibility is jeopardized if you write "We were literally climbing the walls." On the other hand, you might write "He literally got away with murder" and mean it if he killed someone and got away with it. Use *literally* with care.

Loose, Lose: *Loose* is an adjective meaning unrestrained or not fastened. *Lose* is a verb that is the antonym of *win* and *find*.

Majority, Plurality: A *majority* is at least half of the votes cast plus one; a *plurality* is the highest number of votes when there are three or more candidates.

Meantime, Meanwhile: *Meantime* is a noun that refers to an interval between events.

> We will meet at 3:00 this afternoon. In the meantime, prepare your responses to the board's questions.

Meanwhile is an adverb meaning *during* the intervening time.

> Meanwhile, back at the ranch...

You can interchange *in the meantime* and *meanwhile*, but do not write "in the meanwhile."

Media: A newspaper is a medium of mass communication. So are radio, television, and magazines. As a group, it is correct to refer to them as "the media," but be sure to use a plural verb: *media are*. If fortune tellers or a substance used in a lab to culture cells is the kind of medium being discussed, *mediums* is the correct plural.

Myriad: An adjective meaning a large number. Don't write "a myriad of."

Myself: See the entry for I, Me, Myself, p. 139.

Nano-: A prefix meaning billionth or one part in one billion (U.S.). *Nano-* is a scientific term that has been seized upon by nonscientists and often used (incorrectly) to indicate a very small amount (*I didn't consider the alternative for a nanosecond*). Let's leave *nano-* to the scientists.

Nauseated, Nauseous: According to Theodore Bernstein, a person who feels sick is no more nauseous than a person who has been poisoned is poisonous. Though the distinction between the verb *nauseate* and the adjective *nauseous* has all but disappeared in speech, you should observe the difference in writing. Something that makes you feel sick is *nauseous* (*nauseous fumes*); what you feel is *nauseated* (*The fumes nauseated me*).

People, Persons: In general, use *people* for larger groups, *persons* for an exact or small number.

> Eight persons are being held as hostages.

> *The trouble with people is not that they don't know but that they know so much that ain't so.*—Josh Billings

If *persons* sounds affected, try using a more specific noun, such as *commuters*, *residents*, or *visitors*.

Pore, Pour: The verb *pore* means reading or scrutinizing intently, and *pour* means to let flow. The noun *pore* is a minute surface opening, as in the skin of an animal.

> While she was poring over the document, she poured herself a glass of wine.

Predominant, Predominate: *Predominant* is an adjective meaning most common or having the greatest influence or force. *Predominate* is a verb meaning to prevail or to have the greatest influence.

The predominant theme of the parade was patriotism.

The patriotic theme predominated over all others.

Though the adverb *predominantly* is correct, there is no such word as *predominately*.

Principal, Principle: *Principal* functions as both noun and adjective. The noun refers to the head of a school or firm, or to capital that earns interest; the adjective means chief or main. *Principle* is a noun meaning rule or standard.

The principal's principal principle was "Be Prepared for Anything."

Rebut, Refute: The verb *rebut* means to argue against; *refute* to prove incorrect.

Respectfully, Respectively: *Respectfully* means full of respect (*I respectfully disagree*). It may be used in the formal closing of a letter (*Respectfully yours*). *Respectively* means individually in the order given (*Suzanne Johnson and William Campbell were elected president and vice-president, respectively*). Do not sign a letter "Respectively yours."

Shall, Will: This is one instance where the fading of an old grammatical distinction is welcome. Don't worry about rules regarding *shall* and *will*, or *should* and *would*. Just let your ear be your guide.

Stanch, Staunch: *Stanch* means to stop the flow; *staunch* is steadfast, true.

You may need a staunch friend to stanch a bloody wound.

Stationary, Stationery: *Stationary* means fixed in position, not moving. *Stationery* is writing paper and envelopes.

 A good mnemonic is that station<u>e</u>ry is what you need to write l<u>e</u>tters.

Tenant, Tenet: Although both words derive from Latin *tenere* (meaning "to hold") and to the untrained ear may sound similar, the meanings do not overlap. A *tenant* is one who temporarily holds or occupies property (land, buildings). A *tenet* is an opinion or principle held by a person or organization.

The tenants' association drew up a list of tenets for their organization.

That: As an adverb, *that* means to such an extent or degree. *That* is correctly used if what it refers to is clear (*I won't buy a car that old*). A statement such as "I'm not that hungry" is colloquial unless it follows something like "John ate twelve pancakes."

That, Which: Generally, use *that* to introduce restrictive, or defining, clauses; use *which* to introduce nonrestrictive clauses. (See p. 62.)

Restrictive: The pencil that needs sharpening is on my desk.

Nonrestrictive: The pencil, which needs sharpening, is on my desk.

In the restrictive sentence, the pencil is one of several and thus must be further identified; in the nonrestrictive sentence, there is only one pencil, and by the way, it needs sharpening. Note that commas are omitted with restrictive phrases.

Restrictive: *I try to leave out the parts that people skip.* —Elmore Leonard

Nonrestrictive: *Dr. Seuss is remembered for the murder of Dick and Jane, which was a mercy killing of the highest order.*—Anna Quindlen

In the following example, *which* might refer to the word *taxes* or to the entire preceding phrase. Rewrite to avoid such ambiguity.

Unclear: Any attempts to increase taxes, which would harm the recovery...

Clear: Since any attempts to increase taxes would harm the recovery...

 Whenever you write *which*, try substituting *that*. If it doesn't alter the meaning, *that* is probably the better word to use.

That, Who, Whose: Although in earlier versions of *Write Right!* I observed that the rules governing the choice between

that and *who* had been relaxed, I now think we've gone over-board. *That* threatens to obliterate *who*. Using *who* to refer to persons makes them seem more human, and we need all the help we can get in that direction these days. Use *that* to refer to things.

Poor: The students that met me in the classroom...

Better: The students who met me in the classroom...

Use *whose* to refer either to persons or things.

The crowd, whose patience had worn thin...

The building, whose architect won a national award...

There's: The contagion of using the contracted form of *there is* with a plural word has spread from spoken to written language. It's an error whether in speech or writing.

Wrong: There's three reasons...

Right: There are three reasons...

Was, Were: Use *were* when expressing a wish or a condition contrary to fact and when following the words *as if* and *as though*. (See p. 16.)

The silence made it seem as if he were speaking to an empty room.

If it were not for the presents, an elopement would be preferable.—George Ade

Use *was* when expressing a past condition that is not contrary to fact.

If Hortense was guilty, she did not show it.

Whatever, Wherever, Whoever, Whenever: Should they be one word or two? If it's a statement, one word; if it's a question, two.

He does whatever he wants.

What ever made you say that?

Who, Whom:

The irony of the *who/whom* problem is that some avoid *whom* completely because they feel uncertain how to use it.

Wrong: Who does this belong to?

Others use it where it doesn't belong, mistakenly thinking they are being grammatically correct.

Wrong: Whom do you think you are?

The best guide is to substitute a personal pronoun for *who* or *whom*. If *he*, *she*, or *they* fits, use *who* (nominative case); if *him*, *her*, or *them* fits, use *whom* (objective case).

The man who committed the crime...
(**he** committed the crime)

Whom the gods wish to destroy, they first call promising.
—Cyril Connolly   (the gods wish to destroy **them**)

To whom shall I report?   (to **him, her,** or **them**)

For prying into any human affairs, none are equal to those <u>whom</u> *it does not concern.*—Victor Hugo
(it does not concern **them**)

An acquaintance is a person <u>whom</u> *we know well enough to borrow from, but not well enough to lend to.*
—Ambrose Bierce   (we know **him** well enough)

People <u>who</u> *say they sleep like a baby usually don't have one.*—Leo J. Burke   (**they** say)

Paul Brians (see Web Sites, p. 200) suggests that you use *who* if you're still uncertain after trying this replacement test. "You'll bother fewer people and have a fair chance of being right."

Would of: Incorrect usage. Write "would have."

I would have (*not* would of) been on time if I hadn't had a flat tire.

Wreak, Wreck: To *wreak* is to inflict; it is correctly used with *havoc*. To *wreck* is to destroy, so *to wreck havoc* is incorrect. (*To reck havoc* would also be incorrect.)

> Our affinity for language makes us human. We are never better than when we use words clearly, eloquently, and civilly.—David W. Orr

6 Style

To make our words count for as much as possible is surely the simplest as well as the hardest secret of style.
—Wilson Follett

The word *style* means everything from conventions of punctuation and capitalization to how written words convey the writer's personality. I use the term in this chapter to suggest ways to make writing readable and ideas clear.

First, let's take a look at the style that dominates the Internet. With its emphasis on speed and up-to-the-minute currency, online style is the ultimate insider's jargon. Rather than make their writing accessible to the masses, online stylists use language as a gatekeeper: "If you're one of us, you'll be able to handle it," seems to be their view.

But even within this in-your-face, elitist approach, a set of commandments has evolved. These rules embrace the irreverent and the colloquial. They encourage the use of initialisms (FWIW, B2B, LOL) and the creation of imaginative new words: *microserfs* (Microsoft employees), *infobahn* (the information superhighway), and *digerati* (the digital elite).

Online style is beyond the scope of this book. If you work or study within its sphere of influence, you should probably become familiar with the rules enunciated on Web sites and in books on the subject. (See Bibliography.)

Think Before You Write

Writing proceeds more smoothly if you pause before plunging in.

- What do you want to say?

- Who will read it?

Keep coming back to those two elements (message and audience) as you write. Ask yourself if readers will grasp what you've written.

> *It's impossible for a muddy thinker to write good English.*—William Zinsser

"Think of it as elevator talk." That's the advice given to Stanford students learning to write about their work. Someone in an elevator asks what your research is about, and you have to respond in the time it takes to go from the lobby to the fifth floor.

This approach changed one student's paper from "Investigating Cytoskeletal Dynamics in the Development of Epithelial Cell Polarity" into "How Do Cells Know Up from Down?"

Dense, awkward writing detracts from what you want to convey. Confusing writing bogs readers down. Clear, concise writing, on the other hand, speeds readers along.

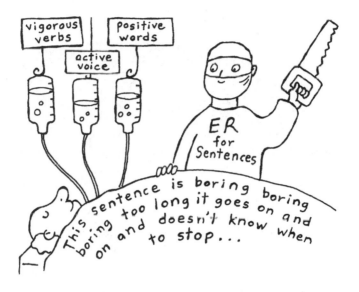

Omit Unnecessary Words

> *If it is possible to cut a word out, always cut it out.*—George Orwell

This rule is increasingly important because word processors encourage verbosity. However, the technology that spreads the disease also provides the cure; revising on a word processor is relatively simple.

Impressive writing doesn't come from long words strung together in convoluted sentences. Writing that's hard to understand is just poorly written, not profound.

> **Wordy:** Our proposal follows the sequential itemization of points occurring elsewhere in your Request for Proposal, wherever possible, to facilitate your review.

> **Translation:** We will follow your outline.

Redundancy and sloppy usage are widespread (see the list of redundant expressions on page 157). "General consensus of opinion" uses four words where only one is correct (*consensus* means collective opinion or general agreement). "Close proximity" is one word too many, since *proximity* means close to. Watch for repetitions in acronyms as well. Write "SAT," not "SAT test," and "ATM," not "ATM machine." The V in HIV stands for virus; the non-redundant phrase is "AIDS virus."

> *The equivalent of junk food for the writer
> is redundancy, and the job of the editor
> is to count calories and impose diets.*
> —Bruce O. Boston

REDUNDANT EXPRESSIONS

added bonus	past history
advance warning	present incumbent
both men and women alike	rarely ever
current status	refer back
end result	regular routine
extra added features	small in size
first time ever	sudden impulse
future plans	sum total
hot water heater	temporary reprieve
join together	tired cliché
joint collaboration	two polar opposites
limited only to	ultimate outcome
may possibly	unexpected surprise
natural instinct	various different
original founder	10 a.m. Friday morning

Think about the meaning of a word. *Unanimous* means having agreement and consent of all; what is added by writing *completely unanimous*? Clutter. How about the ubiquitous *free gift*. Is there any other kind?

Wordy: She estimated attendance at around 500.
Better: She estimated attendance at 500.

Wordy: Chances are that you have probably heard of...
Better: Chances are that you have heard of...
or You have probably heard of...

> *Wherever we can make twenty-five words
> do the work of fifty, we halve the area in which
> looseness and disorganization can flourish.*
> —Wilson Follett

To make twenty-five words do the work of fifty, cut the unnecessary words. Avoid the following redundancies:

- The word *rather* in a sentence with another comparative

  Wordy: It would be safer to destroy the chemicals rather than to store them.
  Better: It would be safer to destroy the chemicals than to store them.

- Leisurely openers such as *There is, There are,* and *It is significant to note that*

  Wordy: There is some evidence that suggests...
  Better: Some evidence suggests...

- *As well as* when used with *both*

  Wordy: The press release was mailed both to employees as well as shareholders.
  Better: The press release was mailed both to employees and to shareholders.

Trim wordy expressions.

Wordy	Trimmed
It is often the case that	frequently
fail to comply with	violate
in the event that	if
be of the opinion that	believe
be in possession of	have
owing to the fact that	since (or because)
the fact that he had arrived	his arrival
on the order of	about
in advance of	before
in spite of the fact that	although
is indicative of	indicates
had occasion to be	was
put in an appearance	appeared
take into consideration	consider
each and every	each (or every)

The best cure for wordiness is to revise. Then go back and revise again. Edit once strictly for spare words. When you think you have pruned every one, look again to see if you missed any. Sometimes when you've stripped a sentence of its padding, you discover that the whole sentence is devoid of ideas and thus expendable.

> *He can compress the most words into the smallest idea of any man I ever met.*
> —Abraham Lincoln

Use Simple Words

Why write "facilitate his departure" when you can write "help him leave"? Does *functionality* mean anything other than *function*? *Specific outcomes and objectives* are probably *goals*. Avoid fancy words and phrases when simpler, more direct ones convey the idea.

> **Stilted:** Per our aforementioned discussion, I am herewith enclosing a copy of...
> **Simple:** As promised, here is a copy of...

> **Poor:** I'll contact you to finalize the agreement.
> **Better:** I'll call at your office to sign the contract.

If the following words appear often in your writing, replace them with their simpler counterparts.

Stuffy	Simple
utilize	use
ameliorate	improve
modification	change
deficiency	lack
preventative	preventive
methodology	method
subsequent to	after

> *Shortening a passage isn't merely a matter of taking words away, but of making sure the remaining words are the right ones—words that do enough work to earn their keep.*—Jack Lynch

Write with Strong Verbs and in the Active Voice

Strong verbs "earn their keep." Pass up colorless verbs in favor of lively ones.

Colorless	Lively
exhibit a tendency to	tend to
conduct an investigation	investigate
make a comparison between	compare
perform an assessment of	assess

The difference between active and passive voice is the difference between *Karen read the report* and *The report was read by Karen.* In the active voice, the subject acts *(Karen read)* instead of being acted upon *(The report was read by...).* The passive voice is wordy and lacks the vigor of the active voice. Changing a sentence from passive to active usually improves it.

Active   *Passive*

Passive: Hazardous chemicals should never be poured into the sink.
Active: Never pour hazardous chemicals into the sink.

Passive: The collision was witnessed by a pedestrian.
Active: A pedestrian saw the collision.

Use the passive voice in the following situations:

- When the thing acted upon is more important than the person performing the action

  The meeting was canceled.

- In technical material

  The test apparatus was divided into two zones.

- Where anonymity of those performing the action is appropriate or unavoidable

  The information was leaked to the press.

Choose the Right "Person" for Your Audience

A decision that's closely related to active or passive voice is whether to write in the first person (*I*, *we*) or the more impersonal third person (*he, she, they*). And should you address the reader as "you" (second person)?

These questions don't have one-response-fits-all answers. In its favor, first-person writing encourages use of the active voice and avoids awkward substitutes for *I* (such as *the author*). Third-person writing puts the writer in the background, which may be appropriate in certain writing; it also avoids being overly familiar.

Readers of scientific or technical writing, where the emphasis is on results, tend to expect an impersonal third-person approach. First-person writing may deflect the reader's attention from the message to the messenger.

Other kinds of writing may call for the more friendly, human tone of first-person writing. This book is an example of first- and second-person writing. What I present is *my* advice, and I'm talking to *you*! Let the nature of the writing and of the audience determine your choice.

Use a Positive Form

Stating things positively starts the reader on the right foot. Watch for the word *not* and see if you can restate the idea more effectively.

> **Negative:** He often did not arrive on time.
> **Positive:** He often arrived late.

> **Negative:** The witness did not speak during the inquest.
> **Positive:** The witness was silent during the inquest.

Try replacing a word or phrase plus *not* with its antonym.

Negative	Positive
did not remember	forgot
was not present	was absent
did not pay attention to	ignored

Reserve the negative form for those instances where it produces the desired effect.

> *Of all noises, I think music is the least disagreeable.*
> —Samuel Johnson

> *I have always been in a condition in which I cannot* not *write.*—Barbara Tuchman

Be Specific and Concrete

Use examples to bring abstract ideas down to earth.

> **Abstract:** The equipment malfunctioned.
> **Concrete:** The camera failed to expose any film.

> **Abstract:** The new health and family programs improved employee performance.
> **Concrete:** Absenteeism was reduced by 40 percent when the company built an employee gym and offered child-care services.

Wherever possible, replace abstract words with concrete ones. Help readers visualize what you're writing about.

Abstract	Concrete
vehicle	bicycle, panel truck
food	pizza, papaya
color	red, chartreuse
emotion	hatred, confusion

Vary Your Sentences

Use sentences of different lengths and types to retain reader interest and to provide relief from monotonous declarative sentences. Open with one of the following:

- With a subordinate clause

  If you want to be a writer, don't listen to any advice given by writers.—Jon Scieszka

  When the student is ready, the teacher will appear.
  —Chinese proverb

- With an infinitive

  To get profit without risk, experience without danger, and reward without work is as impossible as it is to live without being born.—A. P. Gouthey

- With a participial phrase

  Thrusting my nose firmly between his teeth, I threw him heavily to the ground on top of me.—Mark Twain

- With a preposition

  Behind the phony tinsel of Hollywood lies the real tinsel.—Oscar Levant

Notice the rhythm of what you have written. Is it choppy, lively, flowing? Listen to the sound of the words—are there any awkward neighbors like *Our products produced...* or *prevention intervention*? Use rhythm, flow, and contrast to make language and meaning harmonious. Read what you have written out loud; you will discover awkward passages and places where punctuation is needed.

Use Intensifiers with Care

We sometimes rely on the word *very* to convey a strong emotion or lean on words like *incredible* or *unbelievable* to describe a powerful experience. Such words signal sloppy writing—and sloppy thinking. Indeed, intensifier-heavy writing may actually weaken the emotion you wish to convey.

Poor: His contribution was very critical.

Better: His contribution was critical.

Absolute words such as *unique* and *final* stand by themselves; you do not make them more emphatic by adding the word *very*. If a word seems weak without *very*, use another word that doesn't require such buttressing.

Weak	Strong
very stubborn	obstinate, bullheaded
very weak	frail, feeble, fragile
very surprised	astonished, astounded, amazed
very angry	livid, incensed, irate

If you write that something was "incredible," you probably mean that it was amazing or top-notch, not that it was unthinkable or not to be believed. From its origin as a word meaning not to be believed, *incredible* has strayed far afield. It's now loosely used to express amazement—even admiration—rather than skepticism. With a little thought or a look in your thesaurus, you can find a word that comes closer to your meaning.

To describe the extraordinary, focus on what makes it so. Steer clear of words that say what it *isn't* in favor of words that say what it *is*.

Appeal to the senses: how the salsa nips the tongue or the modern concerto assaults the ears. Allow its distinguishing features to evoke an image.

> In autumn, rains return and with them silky verdant grasses, nothing like the color of spring, but a lush, rampant green that makes you understand the urge horses must have to graze. When the trees begin to splatter yellow, russet, bronze, and scarlet over the slopes, the air sharpens to a noon clarity that outlines every leaf.

I wish I could limn the autumn sunsets. Words sound too exaggerated because a literal shower of gold seems to fall over the valley, as if in a myth, forming a veil between me, with my feet on the solid ground, and the glob of live lava sinking in the western distance. The sky goes wild with colors—opal, saffron, dusty blue, copper, ash, blood. ...I hesitate to go on about sunset, that hackneyed oil painting. If only the townspeople would gather at the Porta Colonia parking lot looking out over the valley and give a standing ovation. (Frances Mayes, *In Tuscany*)

Not an *incredible* in the whole passage.

There are legitimate uses of words that express incredulity. If you want to cast doubt on the integrity of a witness or the results of an experiment, you might write about the *incredible testimony* or *unbelievable results*. Legitimate uses of the word *very* also exist, though none come to me at the moment. But do take the time to figure out what you want to say, and choose words that will help you say it.

Edit for Bias

Bias-free language avoids possible offense by substituting alternative terminology. Here are a few guidelines to remove bias from your writing without resorting to awkward wording.

- Do not mention race, gender, age, or disability unless it is pertinent.

- Avoid stereotypes and labels.

- Give parallel treatment (Mr. Waxman and Ms. Stone, *not* Mr. Waxman and Linda).

- Find substitutes for words that may be considered insensitive or confusing, such as masculine pronouns. (See p. 37.)

More detailed suggestions for avoiding bias are presented in two of my books, *Better Letters* and *Rewrite Right!* (see the bibliography).

Become Your Reader

> *I don't think it ever hurts the writer to sort of stand back now and then and look at his stuff as if he were reading it instead of writing it.*—James Jones

Have you brought readers along, step by step? If you present too much information too quickly, readers balk. Build on common ground, on a premise that everyone understands. Proceed from there with digestible bits.

Here's how one writer tackled a difficult subject:

It was about elementary arithmetic, to begin with, and it was not until the second chapter that I as much as got into Arabic numerals, and not until the fourth chapter that I got to fractions. However, by the end of the book I was talking about imaginary numbers, hyperimaginary numbers, and transfinite numbers—and that was the real purpose of the book. In going from counting to transfinites, I followed such a careful and gradual plan that it never stopped seeming easy. (Isaac Asimov, *Opus 100*)

Revisit the questions you asked yourself when starting to write. Have you said what you wanted to say? Did you use as few words as possible? Will your readers still be with you at the end? If your answers are all positive, congratulate yourself on a job well done.

Resources

Frequently Misspelled Words

To differentiate between words with similar sounds (*accept/except*), a brief parenthetical definition follows the first entry. The sound-alike is indented below and then defined at its own alphabetical entry.

Necessary definitions or alternative spellings follow some entries. A list of plurals of foreign words appears at the end of this section.

A

aberration
abridgment
absence
accelerator
accept (receive)
   except
accessible
accessory

accumulate
achievement
acknowledgment
acquiesce
acquittal
adjourn
adolescence
advertisement

aerosol
affidavit
aging
algorithm
align
allotment
allotted
all right

already
anachronism
analogous
analysis
ancillary
anesthetic
annihilate
anomaly
anonymous
antecedent

antihistamine
apartheid
aperture
apparatus
apparel
appraisal
apropos
arctic
arraign
arteriosclerosis

arthritis
asphyxiate
aspirin
assessor
asterisk
attendance
attorneys
autumn
auxiliary

B

balance
ballistic
balloon
bankruptcy
barbiturate
basically
beneficial
benign
bereave
bilateral

bilingual
binary
biodegradable
biopsy
bipartisan
blatant
bloc (group)
bouillon (soup)
  bullion
bourgeois

boutique
boycott
braille
brief
bruise
bullion (gold)
  bouillon
bureaucracy
business
byte

C

caffeine
calendar
calorie
campaign
cannot
captain
carat

carbohydrate
carburetor
Caribbean
carriage
Caucasian
caucus
caveat

ceiling
cellar
cemetery
censor
census
centimeter
centrifugal

cerebral
certain
changeable
charisma
chassis
chauvinist
chiropractor
chlorophyll
chocolate
cholesterol
Christian
Cincinnati
cipher
circuit
cite (quote)
   sight
   site

clothes
cocaine
coliseum (or
   colosseum)
colonel
colossal
column
commitment
commodities
compatible
competent
concurrence
condemn
conductor
conduit
conjugal
Connecticut

conscience
consensus
consortium
continuum
corps
correspondence
counterfeit
coup d'état
courtesy
cousin
cryptic
curtain
cylinder
czar

D

database
debugging
deceive
decibel
deductible
defendant
deferred
depot
depreciate
descend
desiccate
desperate

deterrent
develop
diaphragm
dichotomy
dictionary
diesel
digital
dilemma
dinosaur
disappoint
disburse (pay out)
   disperse

discreet
   (cautious)
discrete
   (separate)
disperse (scatter)
   disburse
dissipate
distributor
doubt
dyeing (coloring)
dying (death,
   expiring)

E

ecstasy
eighth
either
elicit (draw forth)
  illicit
embarrass
emphysema
empirical
encyclopedia
endeavor

entrepreneur
envelop (verb)
envelope (noun)
epitome
equipped
equivocal
errata
erroneous
esthetic (or
  aesthetic)

euthanasia
exaggerate
except (other than)
  accept
exhaust
exhibition
exhilarate
existential
exponential
extraterrestrial

F

facsimile
familiar
faze (disturb)
  phase
feasibility
feature
February
fetus
fiduciary

fierce
flourish
fluorescent
fluoridate
foreign
foreseeable
foreword (in a book)
  forward
forfeit

forward (to the
  front)
  foreword
freight
fulfill

G

gallon
gauge
genealogy
generic
geriatrics
gestalt
ghetto

gorilla (primate,
  animal)
  guerrilla
gourmet
governor
graffiti
grammar

grief
grievance
guarantee
guerrilla (revolutionary)
  gorilla
guess
gynecology

H

hallucinogen

harass

Hawaiian

height

heir

hemorrhage

hertz

hiatus

hierarchy

holistic

holocaust

homogeneous

hors d'oeuvre

hydraulic

hyglene

hypocrisy

I

idiosyncrasy

idle (inactive)

idol (image)

illicit (forbidden)

   elicit

impeccable

impetus

impresario

imprimatur

inadvertent

incessant

incumbent

independent

indictment

indispensable

infrared

innocuous

innuendo

inoculate

intermittent

intravenous

iridescent

irrelevant

irresistible

irrevocable

irrigate

island

J

jeopardize

journey

judgment

junta

K

khaki

kibbutz

kilometer

kilowatt

knowledge

L

label
laissez faire
laser
league
legislature
leisure
leukemia

liable
liaison
libel
license
lieu
lieutenant
lightning

likable
likelihood
liquefy
liquor
logarithm

M

maintain
maintenance
malignant
maneuver
manila
margarine
marijuana
marital
marshal
martial
martyr
Massachusetts
massacre

mathematics
mediocre
megabyte
megawatt
memento
menstruation
metaphor
metastasize
microprocessor
migraine
mileage
milieu
miniature

minuscule
minutiae
miscellaneous
mischievous
missile
misspell
mnemonic
modem
monitor
mortgage
mustache

N

naive
necessary
neither

niece
noxious
nozzle

nuance
nuclear

O

occasion
occurrence
odyssey
ombudsman

omniscient
ophthalmologist
overrun

P

panacea
paradigm
parallel
parameter
paraphernalia
parliament
per diem
peremptory
perennial
peripheral
permissible
personnel
perspiration
pharmaceutical

phase (aspect)
   faze
Philippines
phosphorus
physician
placebo
plebiscite
pneumonia
poisonous
pollutant
polymer
porous
posthumous
precede

preferred
prerogative
prevalent
privilege
procedure
proceed
programmer
prophecy (noun)
prophesy (verb)
protein
protocol
pseudonym
publicly
Puerto Rico

Q

quasi
questionnaire
queue

quiche
quorum

R

rapport
rarefy

rebuttal
recede

receipt
receive

reciprocal
recommend
reconnaissance
recuperate
recurrence

referred
rehearsal
relevant
remittance
renaissance

renege
rescind
resistance
rhythm

S

saccharin (noun)
saccharine (adj.)
sacrilegious
satellite
scenario
schedule
scissors
secretary
seizure
separate
sergeant
siege
sight (vision)
   cite
   site
silhouette

similar
simulate
simultaneous
site (location)
   cite
   sight
skeptical
solar
sophomore
spaghetti
stratagem
strategy
stupefy
subpoena (or
   subpena)
subtle

succeed
superintendent
supersede
surprise
surveillance
syllable
synagogue

T

tariff
thief
threshold
tobacco

tongue
toxin
trafficking
trauma

treasurer
trek

U

ubiquitous
unanimous
unnecessary

unprecedented
usage

V

vacuum
vehicle
vengeance

verbatim
veterinarian
vice versa

vicious
villain

W, Y, Z

waiver
weird
wholly
withheld

woolen
yield
zucchini

Plurals of Foreign Words

Singular	Plural
alumnus (masc.)	alumni (masc. or both masc. and fem.)
alumna (fem.)	alumnae (fem.)
axis	axes
crisis	crises
criterion	criteria
datum	data
medium	media *or* mediums
memorandum	memoranda *or* memorandums
nucleus	nuclei
phenomenon	phenomena
stimulus	stimuli
stratum	strata

Anglicized Plurals

Singular	Plural
antenna	antennas *or* antennae (scientific)
appendix	appendixes
cactus	cactuses
formula	formulas
index	indexes *or* indices (scientific)
prospectus	prospectuses

Glossary

Active Voice: The form of the verb to use when the subject performs the action. See Passive Voice and p. 161.

Adjective: Modifies (describes or limits) a noun or pronoun. It may be a single word, phrase, or clause. See p. 5.

> A _good_ politician is quite as unthinkable as an _honest_ burglar.—H. L. Mencken

Adverb: Modifies a verb, an adjective, or another adverb. May be a single word, phrase, or clause. See p. 6.

> The language of advertising..._profoundly_ influences the tongues and pens of children and adults.—E. B. White

Antecedent: The word, phrase, or clause referred to by a pronoun. In the following example, the pronoun _it_ refers to _book_; thus, _book_ is the antecedent of _it_.

> It occurred to me that perhaps writing a _book_ was not as entertaining an activity as signing the contract to write _it_. —Pete Dexter

Antonym: A word having a meaning opposite to that of another word. *Spicy* is the antonym of *bland; ill* is the antonym of *healthy*. See Synonym.

Appositive: A word or phrase that explains the preceding word or phrase. Since appositives are nonrestrictive, they should be surrounded by commas. See p. 63.

> Alfred Nobel, the Swedish chemist and engineer, received a British patent for dynamite in 1867.

Article: The words *a, an*, and *the*.

Case: The changes in form made in nouns or pronouns to reflect how they are used in a sentence. For example, the noun *children* is changed to *children's* and the noun *person* is changed to *person's* to show possession. Nouns in English once had many case forms, but the only one used today is the possessive. Pronouns, however, continue to change form to show their relation to the rest of the sentence. The three cases of pronouns are nominative, objective, and possessive. See p. 20.

Clause: A group of words that contains a subject and verb. See p. 12. **Coordinate clauses** have the same grammatical rank and are connected by coordinating conjunctions.

> *The wise make proverbs* and *fools repeat them*.
> —Isaac Disraeli

Dependent clauses (also known as **subordinate clauses**) do not express a complete thought.

> *If you can't annoy somebody*, there is little point in writing.—Kingsley Amis

Independent clauses (also called **principal** or **main clauses**) are complete statements that make sense by themselves.

> *There's no money in poetry, but then there's no poetry in money either.*—Robert Graves

Nonrestrictive clauses could be omitted without changing the meaning; they are separated from the rest of the sentence by commas.

> *Practical men, <u>who believe themselves to be quite exempt from any intellectual influences</u>, are usually the slaves of some defunct economist.*—John Maynard Keynes

Restrictive clauses could not be omitted without changing the meaning of the sentence.

> *The man <u>who walks alone</u> is soon trailed by the F.B.I.*
> —Wright Morris

Cliché: An expression that has lost its freshness by being overused. Examples are *conspicuous by its absence, in the final analysis, add insult to injury,* and *it goes without saying.*

Comma Fault: The error in which a comma is the only punctuation between two independent clauses. Rewrite by replacing the comma with a semicolon or period. See p. 57.

Complement: A word or phrase that completes the meaning of the verb. See p. 11.

> *Great artists need <u>great clients</u>.*—I. M. Pei

> *A human being is <u>nothing but a story with skin around it</u>.*
> —Fred Allen

Compound: Consisting of two or more elements. See p. 116. A **compound adjective,** also known as a unit modifier, consists of two or more adjectives modifying the same noun.

> That <u>swarming, million-footed, tower-masted and sky-soaring</u> citadel that bears the name of the Island of Manhattan.—Thomas Wolfe

A **compound sentence** consists of two or more independent clauses.

> I respect faith, but doubt is what gets you an education. —Wilson Mizner

A **compound subject** consists of two or more subjects having the same verb.

> <u>Papa, potatoes, poultry, prunes, and prism</u> are all very good words for the lips; especially prunes and prism. —Charles Dickens

A **compound verb** consists of two or more verbs having the same subject.

> The strong winds <u>tore off</u> roofs and <u>blew down</u> power lines.

Conjunction: A single word or group of words that connects other words or groups of words. See p. 6. **Coordinating conjunctions** connect words, phrases, or clauses of equal grammatical rank: *and, but, or, nor, for,* and *so.*

> Some editors are failed writers, <u>but</u> so are most writers. —T. S. Eliot

Subordinating conjunctions connect clauses of unequal rank (i.e., an independent and a dependent clause). Examples are *as, as if, because, if, since, that, till, unless, when, where,* and *whether.*

> <u>When</u> I am ready to write a book, I write the ending first.
> —Marcia Davenport

Dangling Modifier: A modifier with an unclear reference. See p. 40.

> <u>Taking the elevator to the fifth floor</u>, the room is easy to find.

Double Negative: Two negative words that cancel each other to create a positive meaning. Such usage is incorrect if it is unintended (*You won't hardly believe this*), but may be used for its nuances (*The movie was not without its entertaining moments*). See p. 42.

Gerund: The *-ing* form of a verb that serves as a noun.

> <u>Seeing</u> is <u>believing</u>.

> There must be more to life than <u>having</u> everything.
> —Maurice Sendak

Idiom: A form of expression that, while natural or preferred in a language or region, does not always conform to the rules of grammar or logic. Examples are *rubbing someone the wrong way, taking it easy, stood me in good stead,* and *to make up for.* Though difficult to translate into another language, idioms have a long history of use by good writers.

Infinitive: The form of a verb used with the word *to*.

> Better <u>to remain</u> silent and be thought a fool than <u>to speak</u> out and remove all doubt.—Abraham Lincoln

Split infinitives (words inserted between *to* and the verb) have long been an acceptable way to avoid awkward writing.

> Feel free <u>to utterly disregard</u> this formerly steadfast rule.

Interjection: An exclamation such as *Wow!* or *Cool!*

Misplaced Modifier: A modifier that gives a misleading meaning by being incorrectly placed in a sentence. See p. 39.

> The mayor met informally to discuss food prices and the high cost of living <u>with several women</u>.

Mood: Used by a writer to indicate the mode or tone of an action: Is it factual, hypothetical, commanding? See p.15.

Nonrestrictive Elements: Words, phrases, or clauses that add information not essential to the meaning. See Appositive.

> Theobald Tompkins, <u>who has been our neighbor for twenty years</u>, is moving to Arizona next week.

Noun: A word that names a person, place, thing, quality, or act. See p. 4.

Number: Changes made, such as adding an *s*, to reflect whether a word is singular or plural. See p. 14.

Object: The word or phrase that names the thing acted upon by the verb. Objects are complements; they complete the meaning of the verb. See p. 10.

She visited <u>the ancient cathedral</u>.

A **direct object** names the thing acted upon by the verb.

I bought a <u>book</u>.

An **indirect object** receives the direct object.

I bought <u>Aunt Marie</u> a book.

Participle: A form of a verb that has some of the properties of an adjective and some of a verb. Like an adjective, it can modify a noun or pronoun; like a verb, it can take an object. See p. 18.

> *Success is <u>getting</u> what you want; happiness is <u>wanting</u> what you get.*—Charles E. Kettering

In the following examples, the underlined words are participles (verb forms functioning as adjectives):

<u>glowing</u> coals
<u>grayed</u> collars
<u>run-down</u> heels
<u>whipped</u> cream

Parts of Speech: Nouns, pronouns, verbs, adjectives, adverbs, prepositions, conjunctions, and interjections. See p. 3. In the days of *McGuffey's Reader*, students learned the parts of speech with the help of a jingle.

A NOUN's the name of anything;
As, *school* or *garden*, *hoop* or *swing*.

ADJECTIVES tell the kind of noun;
As, *great*, *small*, *pretty*, *white*, or *brown*.

Instead of nouns the PRONOUNS stand:
Their heads, *your* face, *its* paw, *his* hand.

VERBS tell of something being done:
You *read, count, sing, laugh, jump,* or *run.*

How things are done the ADVERBS tell;
As, *slowly, quickly, ill,* or *well.*

CONJUNCTIONS join the words together;
As, men *and* women, wind *or* weather.

The PREPOSITION stands before
a noun; as, *in* or *through* a door.

The INTERJECTION shows surprise;
As, *Oh!* how pretty! *Ah!* how wise!

Passive Voice: The form of the verb used when the subject is the receiver of the action. See Active Voice and p. 15.

Person: Person denotes the speaker (first person), the person spoken to (second person) or the person or thing spoken of about (third person).

Possessive: Showing ownership; also known as the genitive case. See Case.

He is a sheep in <u>sheep's</u> clothing.—Winston Churchill

Predicate: A group of words that makes a statement or asks a question about the subject of a sentence; a predicate is everything in a sentence except the subject. See p. 9. A **simple predicate** consists of a verb.

You <u>can preach</u> a better sermon with your life than with your lips.—Oliver Goldsmith

A **complete predicate** includes verbs, modifiers, objects, and complements.

You <u>can preach a better sermon with your life than with your lips</u>.—Oliver Goldsmith

Prefix: A word element that is attached to the front of a root word and changes the meaning of the root. See Suffix.

<u>dis</u>belief   <u>in</u>attentive

Preposition: A word or group of words that shows the relation between its object and some other word in the sentence. See p. 7.

The playwright needs a producer who will stick by him <u>through</u> thin and thin.—Louis Phillips

Pronoun: A word that represents or stands in for a noun. See p. 5. **Personal pronouns** are *I, you, he, she, it, they* and their inflected forms (*me, my, your, them,* etc.). **Possessive pronouns** indicate ownership.

The book is <u>mine</u>.

Relative pronouns (*who, whom, which, that, what*) join subordinate clauses to their antecedents. In the following sentence, the relative pronoun *who* joins the clause *sang Irish folk songs* with the antecedent *girl*.

The girl <u>who</u> sang Irish folk songs was the star of the show.

Restrictive Elements: Words, phrases, or clauses that are essential to the meaning. See p. 63.

The joke that gets the most laughs wins the prize.

Run-on: The error of connecting two independent clauses without a conjunction or any punctuation. See p. 56.

Sentence: A group of words that contains at least one subject and predicate and expresses a complete thought. See p. 12. A **simple sentence** consists of subject and predicate (in other words, an independent clause).

My speed depends on the state of my bank account.
—Mickey Spillane

Just sit down at the typewriter and open a vein.—Red Smith

A **compound sentence** consists of two or more independent clauses.

Life is a shipwreck, but we must not forget to sing in the lifeboats.—Voltaire

A **complex sentence** consists of one independent clause and one or more dependent (subordinate) clauses; in the following example, the independent clause is underlined.

New York is the only city in the world where you can be deliberately run down on the sidewalk by a pedestrian.
—Russell Baker

Subject: The part of a sentence about which something is said. See p. 9.

Time flies.

You can identify the subject by asking *what* or *who;* your answer is the subject. (What flies? Time flies.)

Some underlined:people think underlined:they are worth a lot of money because underlined:they have it.—Edmund Fuller

Subordinate Clause: See Clause, Dependent.

Suffix: A word element added to the end of a root or stem word and serving to make a new word or an inflected form of the word. Thus, *-ness* and *-ren* added to *gentle* and *child* create the new word *gentleness* and the inflected word *children.* Other examples of suffixes are mother*hood*, depend*able*, arrange*ment*, end*ed*, and walk*ing*. See Prefix.

Synonym: A word having a meaning identical with or very similar to that of another word. *Shout* is a synonym for *yell; likely* is a synonym for *probable.* See Antonym.

Tense: Tells when an action takes place (present, future, past). See p. 15.

Unit Modifier: See Compound Adjective.

Verb: A word that expresses action, being, or occurrence. See pp. 4 and 14.

Time underlined:flies.

Voice: See Active Voice, Passive Voice.

Bibliography

Alred, Gerald J., Charles T. Brusaw, and Walter E. Olim. *The Business Writer's Handbook*, 6th ed. New York: Bedford/St. Martin's Press, 2000.

———. *The Handbook of Technical Writing*, 6th ed. New York: Bedford/St. Martin's Press, 2000.

Amis, Kingsley. *The King's English: A Guide to Modern Usage*. New York: St. Martin's Press, 1999.

Bates, Jefferson D. *Writing with Precision: How to Write so that You Cannot Possibly Be Misunderstood*. New York: Penguin Books, 2000.

Bernstein, Theodore. *The Careful Writer: A Modern Guide to English Usage*. Rockland, ME: Free Press, 1995.

Boston, Bruce O., ed. *STET! Tricks of the Trade for Writers and Editors*. Alexandria, VA: EEI Press, 1995.

Brians, Paul. *The Great Grammar Challenge*. Alexandria, VA: EEI Press, 1998.

Chapman, Robert L., ed. *Roget's International Thesaurus*, 5th ed. New York: HarperCollins, 1992.

EEI Communications Staff. *STET Again! More Tricks of the Trade for Publications People.* Alexandria, VA: EEI Press, 1996.

Follett, Wilson. *Modern American Usage: A Guide*. New York: Hill & Wang, 1998.

Fowler, H. W. *A Dictionary of Modern English Usage*, 2nd rev. ed. New York and Oxford, England: Oxford University Press, 1983.

Garner, Bryan A. *The Oxford Dictionary of American Usage and Style*. New York: Berkley Books, 2000.

Gibaldi, Joseph. *MLA Handbook for Writers of Research Papers*, 5th ed. New York: Modern Language Assn. of America, 1999.

Gorrell, Donna. *A Writer's Handbook, from A to Z*, 2nd ed. Needham Heights, MA: Allyn & Bacon, 1997.

Hacker, Diana. *A Pocket Style Manual*, 3rd ed. New York: Bedford/St. Martin's Press, 2000.

Hackos, Joann T., and Dawn M. Stevens. *Standards for Online Communications*. New York: John Wiley & Sons, 1997.

Hale, Constance, ed. *Wired Style: Principles of English Usage in the Digital Age*, rev. ed. New York: Broadway Books, 2000.

Harrison, Gwen. *Vocabulary Dynamics*. New York: Warner Books, 1992.

James, Ewart. *NTC's Dictionary of British Slang and Colloquial Expressions*. Lincolnwood, IL: NTC/Contemporary Publishing Company, 1997.

Lederer, Richard, and Richard Dowis. *Sleeping Dogs Don't Lay*. New York: St. Martin's Press, 1999.

Lovinger, Paul W. *The Penguin Dictionary of American English Usage and Style*. New York: Penguin Reference, 2000.

Manhard, Stephen J. *The Goof Proofer/How to Avoid the 41 Most Embarrassing Errors in Your Speaking and Writing*. New York: Macmillan Publishing Co., 1998.

McClanahan, Rebecca. *Word Painting: A Guide to Writing More Descriptively*. Cincinnati, OH: Writer's Digest Books, 1999.

Morris, William, and Mary Morris. *Harper Dictionary of Contemporary Usage*. New York: Harper & Row, 1985.

Pavlicin, Karen, and Christy Lyon. *Online Style Guide: Terms, Usage and Tips*. St. Paul, MN: Elva Resa Publishing, 1998.

Plotnik, Arthur. *The Elements of Expression: Putting Thoughts into Words*. New York: Macmillan Publishing Co., 2000.

Podheiser, Mary Elizabeth. *Painless Spelling*. New York: Barron's, 1998.

Rico, Gabriele. *Writing the Natural Way*, rev. ed. New York: Jeremy P. Tarcher, 2000.

Ross-Larson, Bruce. *The Effective Writing Series: (1) Stunning Sentences, (2) Riveting Reports, (3) Powerful Paragraphs*. New York: W. W. Norton, 1999.

Sammons, Martha C. *The Internet Writer's Handbook*. Needham Heights, MA: Allyn & Bacon, 1999.

Shaw, Harry. *Errors in English and Ways to Correct Them*. New York: HarperCollins, 1993.

Spears, Richard A. *NTC's American Idioms Dictionary*. Lincolnwood, IL: NTC/Contemporary Publishing Company, 1991.

Strunk, William, and E. B. White. *The Elements of Style*, 4th ed. Needham Heights, MA: Allyn and Bacon, 2000.

Sun Technical Publications. *Read Me First: A Style Guide for the Computer Industry*. Palo Alto, CA: Sun Microsystems Press, 1996.

Sutcliffe, Andrea J., ed. *The New York Public Library Writer's Guide to Style and Usage*. New York: HarperCollins, 1994.

Tarshis, Barry. *Grammar for Smart People: Your User-Friendly Guide to Speaking and Writing Better English*. New York: Pocket Books, 1993.

Turabian, Kate L. *A Manual for Writers of Term Papers, Theses, and Dissertations*, 6th ed. Chicago: University of Chicago Press, 1996.

University of Chicago Press. *The Chicago Manual of Style*, 14th ed. Chicago: University of Chicago Press, 1993.

United States Government Printing Office. *Style Manual*, rev. ed. Washington, DC: Government Printing Office, 2000.

Venolia, Jan. *Kids Write Right! What You Need to Be a Writing Powerhouse*. Berkeley, CA: Tricycle Press, 2000.

———. *Rewrite Right! Your Guide to Perfectly Polished Prose*. Berkeley, CA: Ten Speed Press, 2000.

———. *Better Letters: A Handbook of Business and Personal Correspondence*. Berkeley, CA: Ten Speed Press, 1995.

Vitanza, Victor J. *Writing for the World Wide Web*. Needham Heights, MA: Allyn & Bacon, 1997.

Walker, Janice R., and Todd W. Taylor. *The Columbia Guide to Online Styling*. New York: Columbia University Press, 1998.

Walsh, Bill. *Lapsing into a Comma: A Curmudgeon's Guide to the Many Things that Can Go Wrong in Print—and How to Avoid Them*. Chicago: Contemporary Books, 2000.

Wittels, Harriet, and Joan Greisman. *A Handbook of Commonly Misspelled Words*. New York: Grosset & Dunlap, 2000.

Zinsser, William K. *On Writing Well*, 6th ed. New York: HarperCollins, 1998.

Web Sites

The amount of information on the Internet can be daunting, and it sometimes comes in commercial packages primarily designed to sell books and services. Nonetheless, if you are selective in your searches, you will find much to help you.

Although I've explored each of the sites listed below, new ones appear and old ones disappear in the fluid world of the Internet, so I make no claims for completeness or accuracy. But even if a site is no longer available, along the way you may encounter just what you need. Enjoy the process!

Writing Guides

These sites, in addition to presenting useful information about writing (punctuation, grammar, usage) have links to additional sites of possible interest. When looking for help with a particular writing problem, start with one of these.

http://www.wsu.edu/~brians/

Paul Brians of Washington State University created and maintains this site with flair. In addition to the serious stuff, he includes Mr. Gradgrind's answers to rhetorical questions, such as "What is so rare as a day in June," and "Who's afraid of Virginia Woolf."

http://andromeda.rutgers.edu/~jlynch/writing/

Jack Lynch of Rutgers University has packed this site with information. Click on "Guide to Grammar & Style" to explore its many facets. And, should you want to know anything about a moose, click on "Moose Resources." Never let it be said that an English professor doesn't have a sense of humor.

http://www.robinsnest.com

Created and maintained by Robin Nobles, an author and teacher, this site has links to the above two sites, as well as many others of interest to writers.

http://www.theslot.com/

This idiosyncratic site is the work of Bill Walsh of the *Washington Post*. In segments with titles like Carets & Sticks, and Sharp Points, Walsh presents views on writing of special interest to journalists.

http://ccc.commnet.edu/grammar

Charles Darling of Capital Community College maintains this site, which presents half a dozen menus to choose from (e.g., Word & Sentence Level, Ask Grammar, Quizzes, and Index). Includes an extensive list of Notorious Confusables.

http://www.edufind.com/english/grammar/
The Online English Grammar, created by Anthony Hughes, provides free online English grammar resources.

Information About the Web and the Internet

http://www.northernwebs.com/bc
Beginners' Central, where you will find basic information about downloading, advanced search techniques, and so on, plus Myths of the Internet and a glossary.

http://www.about-the-web.com
Topics include avoiding scams, Great Web Sites, glossary, and a free newsletter, "What's New about the Web."

http://www.learnthenet.com/english
Basic information for Web novices.

http://www.help.com
Includes the offer of a free Tweak Freak Newsletter to "show you how to squeeze every last drop of performance out of your system."

http://www.hansenmedia.com
"Your Digital Media Reference Source."

Dictionaries and Glossaries

http://www.yourdictionary.com
Includes definitions and links to online resources, but not as rich a resource as a dictionary in print form.

http://www.acronymfinder.com
Decodes acronyms for you.

http://www.csgnetwork.com/glossary.html
Computer, telephony, and electronics glossary.

http://www.hotwired.lycos.com/webmonkey/guides
Glossary of Internet terms, such as *HTML* and *ethernet*, as well as abbreviations like nrn (no reply necessary) and rotfl (rolling on the floor laughing).

Reference Sites/Research Tools

http://writetools.com/
"A one-stop reference center for anyone who writes, edits, or checks facts." Sources include everything from Almanacs to Zip Codes.

http://www.powerreporting.com/
"Free research tools for journalists" include grammar and style guides.

http://www.thescratchingpost.com/wordsmithshop/writing.html
Extensive information about writing for the World Wide Web.

http://www.sharpwriter.com/
Includes dictionaries, thesauruses, grammar and punctuation guides, quotations (one of the more commercial sites).

Plain Language Sites

The following two sites advocate plain language in writing (hear, hear!).

http://www.plainlanguage.gov
Includes a PDF version of "Writing User-Friendly Documents" and offers an Adobe Acrobat Reader to view this PDF version. Look for "Plain English Handbook."

http://www.adler.demon.co.uk/clarity.htm
This site is maintained by Clarity, a "worldwide lawyers' group campaigning for plain legal language."

All of the Above

www.verbivore.com
Well, maybe not quite "all," but author Richard Lederer has come close to creating an omnipurpose language Web site. A click on "Language Links on the Internet" provides a host of choices: Etymology, Grammar & Usage, Language Columns (e.g., Grammar Lady, Word for Word), Puns, Word Games, Vocabulary Development, Dictionaries; "Other Language Reference Links" leads to yet another layer of word stuff (e.g., slang, clichés, new words, American vs. English usage). It also includes excerpts from Lederer's books and information about his lecture tours.

Index

Also from Jan Venolia

5³/₈ x 7 inches
200 pages

8¹/₂ x 11 inches
192 pages

6 x 9 inches
128 pages

*Available from your local bookstore, or by ordering direct
from the publisher. Write for our catalogs of over
1,000 books and posters.*

TEN SPEED PRESS
Celestial Arts / Tricycle Press

P.O. Box 7123, Berkeley, CA 94707
www.tenspeed.com
800-841-2665 or fax 510-559-1629
order@tenspeed.com